The Hippos of Troy

The Hippos of Troy

Why Homer Never Talked about a Horse

Francesco Tiboni

Archaeopress Archaeology

ARCHAEOPRESS PUBLISHING LTD
Summertown Pavilion
18-24 Middle Way
Summertown
Oxford OX2 7LG
www.archaeopress.com

ISBN 978-1-78969-899-2
ISBN 978-1-78969-900-5 (e-Pdf)

This book is available direct from Archaeopress or from our website www.archaeopress.com

Contents

List of Figures and Tables

Acknowledgements

My love of underwater and naval archaeology has been nurtured over two decades along the shores of Italy, the lakes of the Alps, and the Mediterranean. I am grateful first to my mentors Raffaele De Marinis, Edoardo Riccardi, and Dominique Garcia as well as to Luigi Fozzati and Sebastiano Tusa for allowing me to develop my interest in naval archaeology and to practice, as director of Naval Archaeological Research, on the field.

I have had the privilege of working together with the remarkable group of archaeologists of the Centre Camille Jullian, among which I have to mention Giulia Boetto, Patrice Pomey, Jean-Cristophe Sourisseau, and many other younger colleagues. Great thanks to all of them.

The bulk of this book was written while I was working on my PhD and on different sites around the coasts of Italy and abroad, with the intellectual and practical support of my wonderful wife and colleague, Laura Sanna, who always supported me during these years. I think her help was fundamental to me not only for the correct analysis of the Greek texts, but also for the study of the naval and nautical dimension of the Homeric world.

I want specially to remember and thank Yaacov Kahanov, who showed me unpublished materials from his research, which were very important for the development of my interpretation of the Homeric words.

For discussion, advice and other information I am grateful to Rosie Bonté, Christoph Boerker, Rubens D'Oriano, Irena Radić, Eric Rieth, Jean-Cristophe Sourisseau, Winfried Held, Timothy Gambin, Deborah Cvickel, Stefano Medas, Massimo Cultraro, Massimo Frasca, Raimondo Zucca, Michele Guirguis, Nicola Cucuzza, Maria Cristina Carile, Joaquin Ruiz de Arbulo, Alberto Salas Romero, and many other colleagues with whom I have had the possibility to discuss my topic and research.

I am also grateful to Roberto Petriaggi, Barbara Davidde, Piero Pruneti and Giovanna Corradini, who permitted me to raise the discussion around this research, allowing me to publish articles and papers in their journals, magazines and books.

I owe a great debt to the professional and responsive staff at Archaeopress, particularly Dr David Davison and his colleagues.

Many thanks also to the anonymous readers who read the full manuscript suggesting corrections and giving me a final positive assessment.

Preface

This book sees the light about five years after the first academic paper I wrote on this topic, while I was a PhD student at the Centre Camille Jullian at the University of Aix-en-Provence. However, it is inspired by a keen interest in naval archaeology, cultivated during more than fifteen years of fieldwork and research on ancient wrecks and ships, both underwater and inland.

Over this time, I have had the occasion to collect iconographical and technical data from several different contexts, particularly referring to the pre-archaic world. As I worked through these data and tried to achieve a good comprehension of the naval dimension of the Mediterranean between the Bronze Age and the beginning of the Iron Age, I became increasingly aware of the fact that naval archaeology is usually considered a specialised field, essentially linked to the study of wrecks and submerged contexts, and rarely used in the wider comprehension and the analysis of the social dimension of the ancient peoples living around the Mediterranean Sea.

On the other hand, during these years, I became more and more convinced that ancient texts and iconography are still too often used uncritically in the analysis of the maritime and naval contexts of the ancient Mediterranean, without a proper understanding of the roots of most modern-day interpretations. In this way, many important elements and data can be lost.

This book represents the main result of my attempts to suggest a refocused and more multidisciplinary approach to archaeological research on the naval dimension of the ancient world. This problem feels more and more fundamental, particularly at present, when naval archaeology appears dominated by an excessive focus on technological issues at the expense of research on the main themes and of results.

My approach to the theme of the Wooden Horse of Troy has never been an attempt to understand what the horse could have been in actuality; this book and what it contains it is rather the result of a five year study of the real naval dimension of the Late Bronze Age and Early Iron Age Mediterranean Sea.

Indeed, the possibility of shedding a light on what Homer actually said in his laconic description of the last night of Troy is, in fact, the product of the chance I have had to deeply analyse the naval context of the Mediterranean Sea of that period with a proper naval archaeological approach, that is by performing a wide analysis of all the images, words and wrecks pertaining to that period.

I hope to make a helpful contribution to naval archaeology, but I also intend this work to be sufficiently clear and accurate that archaeologists, historians, and philologists working on Homer and his time find it useful in their own investigations.

Introduction

To deal with the Homeric epics is to engage with one of the most complex and dangerous topics of the entire modern culture, as these narrations represent the cornerstone on which western civilisation is built.[1]

Conventionally located chronologically between the 13th and the 11th centuries BCE, the Trojan War represents the very first historical appearance of Greece, even though we lack any direct evidence of its precise context.[2] What was narrated by Homer took place in an age of heroes, when kings and princes ruled wide lands from their palaces and sailed the sea to enlarge their sphere of influence. The vivid narrations made by the ancient author of the events of a period that we still call the beginning of 'The Dark Age of Greece'[3] serve to highlight all the more the limits of our present knowledge of where and when all these things happened, assuming they do have a historical basis. The shade that covers the ill-defined period that, after the Trojan War, ends with the migrations that laid the foundations for Greek culture of the historical era, still affects our ability to understand the real dimension of the Homeric epics.

Turning to ancient Greek historians, we can reasonably argue that the events of the Trojan War were first given a factual dimension in the 5th century BC,[4] with the Greek historian Herodotus' statement that those events occurred around eight centuries before the time he was writing. In the same century, as noted by Dickinson, 'it is symptomatic [...] that Thucydides, in his famous account of the past of Greece, found it easier to calculate the dates when the Boeotians and Dorians supposedly moved into southern Greece by reckoning downwards from the Trojan War',[5] thus demonstrating that, although unimpressed by the so-called 'age of heroes', that author believed that the remote traditions of the Trojan war contained truth.

This idea of a factual basis for the events narrated by Homer, while widely accepted,[6] is still debated. Some scholars plausibly refuse to consider the Greek bard as a proper historical source. Following the road defined by Moses Finley,[7] and after George Grote's warnings not to confuse myths with historical facts,[8] they underline how Homer is indeed a poet and a storyteller.[9] That both the Iliad and the Odyssey must be considered as merely literature appeared clear also to some ancient authors, as indeed was noted by Finley, 'to those who called Homer the teacher of Hellas, Plato replied: Yes, he is "first and most poetical among the tragic poets'.[10]

1 Ieranò 2013: 11.
2 On this topic, among the others, Kline 2018, Strauss 2006, Latacz 2004.
3 Whitley 1991: 5.
4 Shapland, Fitton 2019: 172.
5 Dickinson 2006: 1.
6 Shapland, Fitton 2019: 179-81; Cline 2018: 103; Boardman 2014: 25.
7 Finley 2002.
8 Grote 1856: iv-xii.
9 Ieranò 2015: 11-13; D'Agostino 2007.
10 Finley 2002: 11. The author also noted that '*the philosopher Xenophanes had protested that* 'Homer and Hesiod have attributed to the gods everything that is disgraceful and blameworthy among men: theft, adultery, and deceit" (Finley 2002: 11).

In the absence of indisputable evidence, it appears plausible that Homer used a sort of literary license to mix together different peoples, different events, as well as different centuries of intermittent wars to create his epics;[11] as stated by Susan Sherrat 'it is inconceivable that the Trojan War motif, which forms the essential background of both epics, could have been invented out of nothing in the eighth century'.[12] In the deafening silence of any written source, archaeology is our sole guide.

Although there is still no direct way of relating archaeology and poetry, a number of modern authors[13] consider increasingly clear that Homeric narrations relate to the world of the Bronze Age of the eastern Mediterranean region. The siege of Troy, as described in the Iliad, clearly recalls the city sieges as recorded in the Levantine tradition,[14] as well as those depicted on the silver 'Siege Rhyton' of *c.*1600 BC, discovered by Schliemann in one of the shaft graves at Mycenae.[15] According to these scholars, we can also find interesting evidence pertaining to the Homeric world from the excavation held at Hissarlik, the site of the presumed Troy,[16] as well as in the Hittite 'Alaksandu Treaty' or in the 'Tawagalawa Letter', recently deciphered.[17]

With regard to the Trojan Horse, both these sources, the Hissarlik excavations and the Hittite texts, do provide us with some useful elements to understand why, when he referred to the cunning used by the Achaeans to conquer Troy at the end of the siege, Homer never spoke of a giant wooden simulacre of a horse.

During the 1995 campaign, in the $VIIb_2$ layer of the citadel, archaeologists discovered the very first, thus far the sole, Bronze Age object with a reliable inscription found at Troy.[18] Dated to *c.*1100 BC,[19] it is a small bronze disc, about two cm in diameter, inscribed both sides with a hieroglyphic script in use in Bronze Age Anatolia. Once deciphered, it appeared clear that this object was in origin a seal, with a name on each side, one masculine and the other feminine, and that it must have belonged to a scribe.

The presence of a scribe is usually associated with the presence of a centre of administration, and Troy appears to have been one of these centres. Even though we have no direct evidence for the presence of any archive in the citadel, it is likely that in the excavated citadel at Hissarlik there was such a structure, 'traces of it would have been destroyed when the mound was levelled to build the temple of Athena'[20] in the mid-7th century BC.

The importance of Troy as the main centre of its area, as recently supposed on the basis of some Hittite documents[21] appears to be confirmed also by the reading of some cuneiform records, where we can find clues about Troy's involvement in the events of the Bronze Age of the eastern Mediterranean. The archives of the Levant provide evidence that, at least in

[11] Cline 2018: 101-3.
[12] Sherrat 2010a: 5.
[13] Shapland, Fitton 2019: 179-81; Cline 2018: 103; Boardman 2014: 25; Sherrat 2010a.
[14] Liverani 2017: 122-29.
[15] Shapland, Fitton 2019: 180-81.
[16] Shapland, Fitton 2019: 143-70; Cline 2018: 67-99; Hertel 2001: 35-93.
[17] Shapland, Fitton 2019: 174-79; Cline 2018: 51-64; Beckman, Bryce, Cline 2011: 101-22.
[18] Shapland, Fitton 2019: 173.
[19] Cline 2018: 92.
[20] Shapland, Fitton 2019: 174.
[21] Cline 2018: 51-54.

the Bronze Age, the Hittite empire and the Mycenaeans from *Ahhiyawa*, the Hittite name for mainland Greece and its islands,[22] were in conflict, and that one of the citadels involved in these conflicts was *Wilusa*. The possibility that *Wilusa* might be identified with Troy came in 1998, when David Hawkins deciphered the hieroglyphic inscription carved on the Karabel relief,[23] giving the fixed point that made it possible to locate the capital of the land of *Arzawa*, the Hittite centre of *Apasa*, in Ephesus, and the land of *Wilusa* in the Troad. 'The only site known in the Troad large enough to have been its administrative centre in the Bronze Age is Hissarlik. Wilusa and Ilios are thus one and the same'.[24]

Some cuneiform texts from Anatolia provide information about the relationship between the Hittite rulers and the Mycenaean princes of the Bronze Age.[25] Among these, the most interesting appears to be the so-called *Tawagalawa letter*, a clay tablet preserved from a group of three, carved in cuneiform symbols, which gives an account of a correspondence between an unnamed Hittite king and the king of *Ahhiyawa*.[26] In this document, attributed to Hattusili III (1267-1237 BC), the king of Hatti writes to the king of *Ahhiyawa* referring to him as 'his brother'[27] and discusses a possible conflict, rather a simple 'diplomatic issue',[28] involving the Hittites and the people of *Ahhiyawa*, that is the Mycenaeans.

Although surely appealing, the hypothesis to identify this conflict between the Hittites and the people of Ahhiyawa with the Trojan war can be neither confirmed or refuted. Whatever the truth, however, this letter does provide important clues for the correct interpretation of what Homer narrated when reporting the end of the ten-year siege at Troy.

Strictly linked to the world of the Bronze Age Levant, we can plausibly argue that the Homeric narration was grounded in the diplomatic and military customs and practices of that time, which involved, in the case of a defeat in a fight or a war, the payment of a tribute.[29] Some ancient texts[30] testify that the practice of tribute bearing and princes' gifts was common in the Bronze Age Levant, and also involved the area of Anatolia during the early first Millennium BC. As noted by Oscar White Muscarella concerning the 8th century BC 'it is known from Neo-Assyrian texts that subject peoples gave as tribute [...] gold, silver, tin, ivory, camels [...], objects that they acquired by trade or tribute. That is, they gave the Assyrian king what he wanted and expected'.[31]

Therefore, despite the great number of theoretical and philosophical discussions around the meaning of the Wooden Horse, from Pausanias to modern-day scholars, it is more likely that the deception planned by Athena might have been conceived within the framework of the customs and practices proper to the war and diplomacy of the time. Whatever that time was: the second millennium BCE of the presumed Trojan War, or the 8th century BC of Homeric Greece.

[22] Beckman, Bryce, Cline 2011: 4.
[23] Hawkins 1998.
[24] Shapland, Fitton 2019: 179.
[25] Beckman, Bryce, Cline 2011.
[26] Beckman, Bryce, Cline 2011: 101-22.
[27] Cline 2018: 61.
[28] Beckman, Bryce, Cline 2011: 121.
[29] Uberti 2005: 41-96; Canckik-Kirschbaum 2003: 31-39.
[30] Hoftijzer, Van Soldt 1998.
[31] Muscarella 1998: 156.

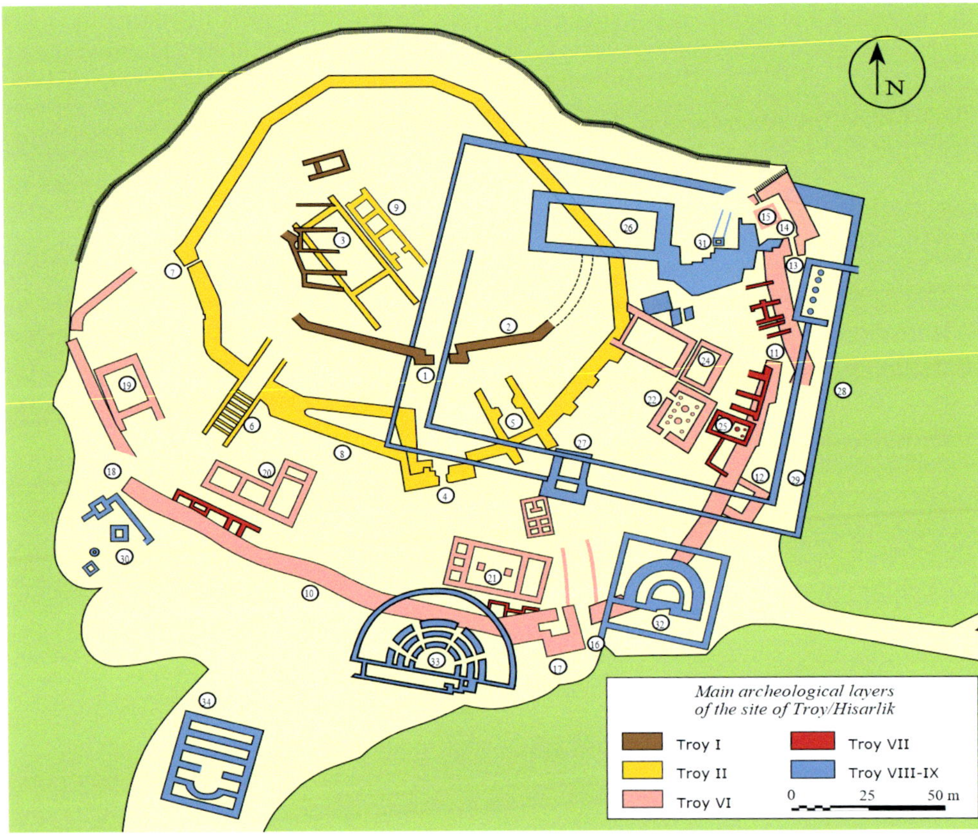

Figure 1. The archaeological site of Hissarlik/Troy - plan.

Following Muscarella, it is more likely that in order to fake their surrender, the Achaeans pretended to give the Trojan (or in the context of the 8th century BC, Phrygian) king what he wanted and expected. And what he wanted could not have been a giant wooden statue in the shape of a horse.

Archaeology at Troy

The idea of a factual basis for Homer's narration may rest on the possibility of identifying the real site of Troy, usually identified with Hissarlik (Figure 1).[32] So, before analysing in detail what Homer said when he spoke of the Trojan Horse, it must be noted that, since the first identification of the historical Troy made by Schliemann, several scholars have investigated the site of Hissarlik in search for the archaeological evidence of the Trojan War.

Two years after Schliemann's death in 1890, architect Wilhelm Dörpfeld started a two-year excavation of the site, between 1893 and 1894,[33] during which he located, on the top of the

[32] Latacz, J. 2004:15-117.
[33] Dörpfeld W., 1902.

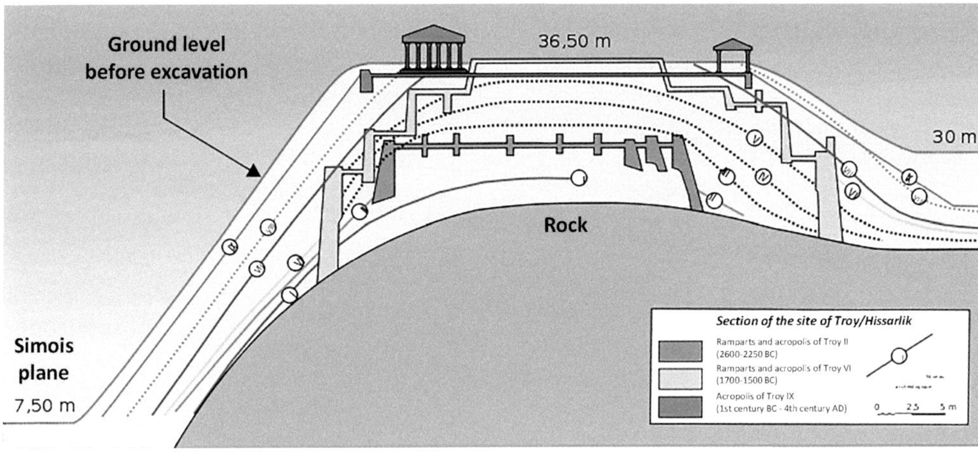

Figure 2. The archaeological site of Hissarlik/Troy – section.

citadel of Hissarlik, the layers of the so-called Troy VI (Figure 2). The presence of a series of fortifications, walls and towers led him to identify this layer, Troy VI, with the Troy narrated by Homer, as suggested, for instance, by the presence of an eight metre high tower, part of a great wall, clearly recalling what was narrated by the ancient bard in the sixteenth book of the Iliad[34]

> τρὶς μὲν ἐπ' ἀγκῶνος βῆ τείχεος ὑψηλοῖο
> Πάτροκλος [...]
>
> Thrice did Patroclus set foot upon a corner of the high wall [...]

The upper layer of Troy VI investigated by Dörpfeld, labelled Troy VIh, appeared to be the richest phase of the city, with its big palace and several elements, particularly ceramic sherds, testifying to a close commercial relationship with the Mycenaean world, possibly proof of the historical friendship between the Mycenaean and the Trojans before the abduction of Helen[35].

The presence of a layer with strong evidence of fires and destruction allowed the scholar to state that Troy VI must have been abandoned after a war, that is, according to Dörpfeld, after the Mycenaean conquest.

Some years later, in the years 30 of the twentieth century, Prof. Blegen could demonstrate, during the new campaigns of research arranged on the site by the University of Cincinnati, that those proofs of war and conquest were in fact the indisputable signs of an earthquake. Although, according to Dörpfeld, the long dispute on the existence of Troy and its site had come to an end with the identification of Troy VIh, some thirty years later, Carl Blegen could demonstrate that the sequent phase of the citadel, labelled Troy VIIa, did not show any evidence of the presence of a new people at Hissarlik. The archaeological record of potteries and finds investigated in Troy VIIa was not to be read as the result of a sudden interruption of the Trojan culture, rather the reconstruction of a crumbled city, pertaining to the same

[34] Homer, *Iliad*, XVI 702-3.
[35] Cline 2018: 80.

cultural framework. Further, according to the author, this layer could have been named Troy VIi rather than Troy VIIa, although he decided to 'preserve the old terminology' to avoid possible confusion.[36]

In particular the presence of Mycenaean potteries together with local Trojan imitations of Mycenaean forms in the layer of Troy VII allowed Blegen to exclude the idea of a sudden change of the cultural actors living in Troy VIh and Troy VIIa, as well as the possibility that the end of Troy VI was consequence of a conquest. 'It seemed more likely that the Mycenaeans were still in a commercial relationship with the Trojans'[37] during the whole life of Troy VIIa, which lasted for about a century and a half.

In addition, Blegen found several proofs of a possible earthquake on the site, particularly thanks to the examination of the fallen walls, so that at the end of his research, he stated 'we are almost sure that the end of the city could be attributed to a big earthquake'.[38] The geo-archaeological examination of the archaeological record corroborated what was reported by Blegen.[39]

As for Troy VIIa, the excavations held by Blegen led to the discovery of a great number of proofs of a violent destruction of the city, among which widely diffused evidence of fires, human skeletal remains, and archaeological contexts of destruction were all compatible with a war scenario like that narrated by Homer.[40] On the basis of the analysis of the ceramic records, particularly of the Mycenaean imports, Blegen dated this destruction to 1260-1240 BC. In this interpretation, sudden ruin appeared to be followed by a rapid and partial reconstruction of the city,[41] which he labelled Troy VIIb1, and then by a phase of abandonment. This latter, labelled Troy VIIb2, marked the end of the Bronze Age occupation of the site, at the end of the 12th century BC.[42]

After Blegen's analysis of the site, debate on the dating of the destruction of Troy VIh flourished among scholars, and as well pointed out by Eric Cline, 'some of them have recently proposed to locate this event between 1130 and 1100 BCE'.[43] However, following Penelope Mountjoy's deep study of the pottery found during the excavation held by Blegen, it seems more likely that the date of the end of Troy VI h corresponds to *c.*1300 BC. Mountjoy's study also confirms the idea of the possible earthquake as the cause for the abandonment of Troy VIh.[44]

The identification of the Troy of Homer with the layer labelled Troy VIIa has been recently revived by Manfred Korfmann of the University of Tubingen on the base of new scientific proofs. Korfmann, who has directed important excavations at the site between 1998 and the early 2000s, has had the possibility to investigate not only the citadel of Troy, but also a substantial portion of the lower city by means of new technologies. His discoveries, which also

[36] Blegen C.W., 1963: 145. The idea to identify Troy VIIa with a supposed Troy VIi is reflected even in Manfred Korfmann interpretation of the site of Hissarlik as clearly stated in Korfmann M., 2004 and *2003*: 5-14.
[37] Cline 2018: 84
[38] Blegen C.W., Caskey J.L., Rawson M., 1953: 331.
[39] The idea of the big earthquake was in fact supported by Rapp (Rapp: 1982: 55-6).
[40] Blegen C.W., Caskey J.L. Rawson M., 1958:11-12; Blegen 1963: 162.
[41] Mountjoy P.A. 1999b
[42] Cline 2018: 89.
[43] Cline 2018: 86.
[44] Mountjoy P.A., 1999a

include a probable moat, evidence of fires, and remains of weapons and unburied skeletons, have shed a new light on the site of Troy. According to Korfmann most of the elements excavated on the site permit stating that Troy VIh shows no cultural break with Troy VIIa, while it is possible to identify evidence of fire and destruction between Troy VIIa and VIIb. This evidence, all suggesting a war scenario, can be dated, in accordance with what was proposed by Mountjoy, to around 1180 BC.[45]

While on the one hand, some of the elements discovered by Korfman seem to permit proposing the identification of Troy as Wilusa,[46] the new date suggested for the destruction of Troy VII, not widely accepted, introduces the possibility to create a link between the end of the city and the Sea Peoples.[47]

Was it a horse?

To understand why, as we are going to demonstrate, when describing the end of Troy and the Achaean conquest of the city after a ten-year siege, Homer never talked about a gigantic wooden-horse proceeds from the precise identification of the site of Troy. However, it should be noted, before we begin our journey, that over the years many scholars have tried to identify what the horse could have been in reality, and to relate it to the ruins of Hissarlik.

While many authors, following the idea of Pliny The Elder, according to whom[48]

> *equum (qui nunc aries appellatur) in muralibus machinis Epium ad Troiam invenit*
>
> Epeius at Troy invented a war machine to surpass the walls named horse (now we call it battering ram)

have interpreted the contrivance as a primitive battering ram used to break the walls, on the other hand, some scholars have tried to figure out how a gigantic wooden horse could have been built to host all the heroes needed for a raid.[49]

Furthermore, following Blegen's discovery of the proofs of the earthquake, Fritz Schachermeyr proposed to interpret the Trojan horse by linking it to the way that Homer describes the earthquake generated by the beating of the horse's hooves on the ground, by divine intervention of Poseidon.[50]

In 2009, Joaquin Ruiz de Arbulo first proposed, on the base of the analysis made by Austin[51] of Vergil's description of the horse, to identify the horse with a sacred and ritual boat. According

---

[45] Korfman theory about the identification of Troy was discussed in the early 2000s and firmly rejected by one of his colleagues at Tubingen, Frank Kolb in 2002. On this topic, among the others see Cline 2018: p. 98-9.

[46] Particularly the moat and some elements like the golden seal with the inscription cited above. On this topic see Cline 2018: 92-9.

[47] The problem of the correct identification of the Sea Peoples is nowadays strongly debated among the scholars. On this topic Cline E.H., O'Connor D. 2012; Sandars N., 1985. It is noteworthy that the Achaeans have often been included among the Sea Peoples.

[48] Pliny The Elder, *Naturalis Historiae*, VII.56.

[49] Jones, J. W. 1970, Rand, H. 2015.

[50] Schachermeyr F., 1950: 189-203.

[51] Austin 1950.

to the scholar, in fact, we can imagine a ritual ship, decorated with a horse figurehead, left on the beach as a gift for the deities. The boat, likely a processional boat, with wheels, must have been very similar to those still visible on the depictions of the ritual processions for Dionysus, displayed on some black-figured vases of the Classical Greece.[52]

This reading was, as we will see, the closest one to the correct interpretation of what Homer actually said. The bard, in fact, never described the use of any war-machine, any gigantic wooden horse, and also never referred to a sacred or to a ritual boat. He has only spoken of a *hippos ship*, a merchant-ship, used in its standard way, that is according to maritime rules and the customs of the Mediterranean of the Late Bronze Age/Early Iron Age.

[52] Ruiz de Arbulo, 2009: 549.

The Naval Dimension of Homer

Although describing an Age of Heroes, Homer did not present to his audience only simple narratives of heroic and historical events; instead, he concentrated on themes. Thus, the *Iliad* does not offer a complete account of the Trojan War, but rather details certain events that took place next to Troy's city walls, and in particular events that were 'dominated by the wrath of Achilles, as stated in the first line of the poem itself'.[1] Homer's *Odyssey*, meanwhile, describes the journey home of one of the heroes after the war, albeit in a discursive narrative that provides much information concerning the antecedents to the war, as well as its progress, and which this has no strictly historical and linear approach.

While much knowledge and memory of the Trojan War must initially have circulated in oral tradition, these events were first set down in writing before the end of the eight century BC,[2] at which time 'the Greeks of the Homeland had learned to write again, a product of their renewed relations with the Near East'.[3] As such, and for all that we clearly lack any strictly historical detail about the 'real' events of the Trojan War, the verses by Homer nonetheless provide us with certain information about the cultural background of the Trojan War — or at least, the context in which this war was narrated.

As noted by a number of authors,[4] when we think about the so-called 'Homeric society' of the eighth century BC, we should seek to envisage a relatively poor but nonetheless ambitious society that held on closely to recollections of a mighty and heroic past, and that sought to create strong links between the present, and the events and cultures of the Bronze Age. The new-born Greek society of the Early Iron Age seems to look for her glorious ancestors by turning to the Bronze Age, to the era of both the Minoan and the Mycenaean cultures, and to the competition with the other eastern actors for the control of the eastern routes of the Mediterranean. This research of a noble ancestry underlies for instance the choice by Homer to cite in the Iliad, among the heroes involved in the Greek expedition to Troy, the mythic king of Crete Minos, the first Greek known to have established a straight control on the eastern Mediterranean sea , as well as that to list a number of different Achaean princes and rulers among the Greeks that move to the Trojan shores at the beginning of the Iliad.

Memory, together with evidence of the physical remains of Bronze Age Greece, in fact provided the background for works of poetry, although depictions of these events were often embellished 'by appeal to divine or heroic intervention'.[5] Thus, we can be reasonably certain that some kind of Greek military activity occurred in north-western Anatolia during the Late Bronze Age[6], and that this in all likelihood involved some Greek actors. But while in light of this historical context, we might expect a great battle or a war fought in land rather than a naval battle, we know in fact that the very first naval battle known for the whole ancient

1 Boardman 2014: 25.
2 Rossi 1977; Hedreen 1995: 153; Reber 2007: 25.
3 Boardman 2014: 25.
4 Janni 1996, Mark 2005, Boardman 2014.
5 Boardman 2014: 25.
6 Janni 1996: 7; Boardman 2014: 25; Baldacci 2017: 27.

history dates to the 6th century BC,[7] the long-lasting siege of the city of Troy as described in the Iliad seems arguably to fall more closely within the war culture of the Levantine area for the Bronze Age. As Mario Liverani has argued, in the Levant, in fact, 'the sieges are very frequent, and we can say that they are the rule. A campaign may not involve any great battle, but the siege of a city is always present'[8] if we analyse military history in the Levant at this time.

On the other hand, as Pietro Janni has pointed out, 'even though we do not have any naval battle at Troy, we must bear in mind that the besiegers reached Troy by sea, and that the sea will be the background [...] for the greatest, the most archetypical and the very first, in any sense, maritime tale: The Odyssey'[9]. Thus, while lists of princes and ships from the 'Catalogue of the ships' given in Book Two of the Iliad recall the environmental and geo-political situation of the Mycenaean Archipelagos of the Bronze Age,[10] from an archaeological perspective, the presence of the sea as the main geographical context for a poem devoted to the creation of the Greek Ethos by means of the transformation of a man into a hero, can be read in light of a desire on the part of the poet to create a link with the glorious past of his people, as discussed above. As well pointed out by Thomas Tartaron, 'in the characters and places of the post-Bronze Age Odyssey, both realistic and fantastical, we may discern traces of the Mycenaean seafarer's phenomenology'.[11]

In both cases, the link between Homer's narratives and the importance of the role played by the sea for the creation of the Greek cultures of the Early Iron Age as a direct descendant from the Minoan and Mycenaean glorious past are evident.

Moreover, it seems likely that the events of the Trojan War, as narrated by Homer, must have continued to circulate orally until at least the eighth century BC, especially amongst the inhabitants of those islands and archipelagos that were home to the great Mycenaean civilization, and thus inhabited by people who were well aware of their distinguished maritime past, which was 'still visible through its ruins'.[12] Many of the people amongst whom these oral poems continued to circulate would have been extremely familiar with the sea, being sailors and fishermen who lived in small villages on the islands and littoral of Greece, and who could understand the naval dimension of Homer's texts far more easily than a modern-day reader. As more than one scholar has noted, the way in which Homer used to talk about the sea and about ships is also demonstrative of how familiar these topics would have been to his audience.[13]

The nautical dimension of the Homeric world

Even though 'the Greeks, of Indo-European origin, entered their eventual homeland from the north',[14] it seems clear that the Homeric epics, which were first composed during the

[7] Gras 2000.
[8] Liverani 2017: 123.
[9] Janni 1996: 7.
[10] Tartaron 2013: 212-84.
[11] Tartaron 2013: 9.
[12] Boardman 2014: 24.
[13] Kurt 1979: 219; Janni 1996: 77.
[14] Boardman 2014: 24.

Figure 3. Iconography of the first Mycenaean galleys of the Mycenaean/ Achaean group as defined by Shelley Wachsmann: the Kynos Ship, Late Helladic IIIC.

Geometric phase, would equally have permeated a culture that was still characterised by a strong post-Mycenaean naval dimension.[15] As has been widely argued,[16] analysis of the naval iconography of the period permits us to interpret the ships of Geometric Greece as direct descendants of those Bronze Age ships belonging to the Mycenaean/Achaean group defined by Shelley Wachsmann (Figure 3).[17] Herman T. Wallinga has further noted that after the collapse of the Near-Eastern regional system of the Late Bronze Age, which dates to the twelfth century BC,[18] at least with regards to the Levant, 'there is no argument in favour of the hypothesis that there was continuity in nautical techniques and skills between the LBA and this period [while we can read] some correspondence between some pictures of the Aegean',[19] particularly with regard to sea-going galleys.

At the dawn of what might arguably be termed 'proper' Greek maritime culture, the two existing ship-types of the Bronze Age Aegean, namely merchantmen and men-of-war, both of which were first attested in the mid-second millennium BC,[20] began to evolve, resulting in a standardised type of hulls. In the case of the merchantmen, this meant an increase in shape and dimension of the hull due to a need for the vessels to take on board a larger crew of about twenty oarsmen. In around the eighth century BC, we find the first reference to εικοσόρος by Homer in the Odyssey.[21]

[15] Treziny 1980: 33-34.
[16] Morrison, Williams 1968: 12-42; Casson 1971: 43-53; Gray 1974, ch. G; Wallinga 1995: 38-43; Pomey 1997: 64-68.
[17] Wachsmann 1998: 123-58.
[18] Wachsmann 1995: 15-21.
[19] Wallinga 1995: 37.
[20] Pomey 1996: 137.
[21] Homer, *Odyssey* IX.322-323.

Figure 4. Image of a 'ship of fifty oars' from a Greek vase of the end of the 8th Century BC.

Figure 5. Image of early Greek warships with two banks of oarsmen.

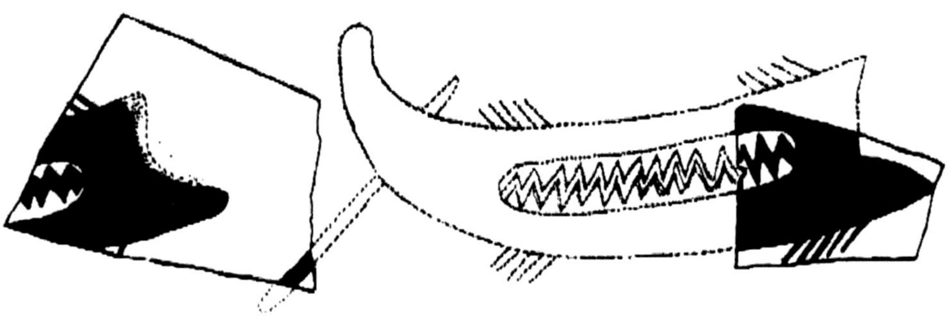

Figure 6. The ship depicted on the Middle Helladic fragment from Volos.

> τὸ μὲν ἄμμες ἐίσκομεν εἰσορόωντες
> ὅσσον θ' ἱστὸν νηὸς ἐεικοσόροιο μελαίνης,
> φορτίδος εὐρείης, ἥ τ' ἐκπεράᾳ μέγα λαῖτμα:
>
> and as we looked at it we thought
> it as large as is the mast of a black ship of twenty oars,
> a merchantman, broad of beam, which crosses over the great gulf;

During a window of time typically dated to between 900 BC and 525 BC, the pre-classical men-of-war also began to expand to increase the number of crew that could be taken on-board, largely to improve speed and manoeuvrability. By the eighth century BC, these vessels can be found referred to as πεντηκοντέροι, 'ships with fifty oars' (Figure 4).

According to the iconographic record,[22] particularly with regards to the warships, the increase in the number of oarsmen did not automatically lead to the decision to lengthen and widen the hulls.[23] Instead, the Greek shipwrights, at least as they are depicted on vases and wall paintings, seem to have adopted different solutions, such as the creation of an outrigger frame and rowing bench (*παρεξειρεσία* and *θρανος*), which made it possible for a large number of oarsmen to board a vessel that nonetheless still featured a fast, agile hull (Figure 5).

In the space of just a few decades, the transformation of warship morphology was virtually completed, with the introduction of a bronze-sheeted ram at the prow that could effectively transform the vessel itself into a weapon intended to fight at sea.[24] In terms of the technological developments made to ships, even though we lack direct evidence of Greek wrecks dating up to the Archaism,[25] it is nonetheless possible to form an idea of how ships were built by analysing the iconographic records in the light of the ancient texts and pictorial evidence. Through these, it is possible to trace, albeit tentatively, the development of both warships and merchant ships between the Late Bronze Age and the Geometric period.

The very first purely Greek depiction of an oared ship (Figure 6) comes from Volos, on Thessaly, and dates to the Bronze Age.[26] Here, on a Middle Helladic fragmented vase that was found in 1956, two ships are depicted, both orientated to the right, and it is possible to attempt to reconstruct their form based on an analysis of the ceramic shreds. The better-preserved of these images depicts a hull on which can be seen a prominent ram, together with part of the bow, while on the side of the ship a decoration with a zig-zag pattern can be identified that recalls the decoration featured on at least one of the ships from the Early Cycladic 'frying pan'.[27] The image also features a series of line on one side, next to the prow, which appears to

[22] Wallinga 1996: 36-37; Morrison, Williams 1968: 12-42, pls. 1-7.
[23] Wallinga 1995: 36.
[24] Walling 1995: 37; Basch 1986.
[25] The Middle Bronze Age Boat of Mitrou, Central Greece, does not provide us with any information about the hull (Van De Moortel, 2012), as it impossible to really gain an idea of the boat's construction from the extant remains. The only traces that remain from this vessel appear to recall those of the Neolithic boat of Dispilio (Marongou 2003), with the traces left in the soil by the wood in the soil indicating that it was constructed as an 'expanded logboat' (McGrail 1985), with monoxylic wood at the centre that functioned as the ship's keel, and planks added on the two sides. This particular construction is attested elsewhere, for instance, in the Zambratija wreck (Boetto et alii 2012), an LBA-EIA boat dated to the tenth century BC and discovered in northern Croatia.
[26] Morrison, Williams 1968: 7.
[27] Johnstone 1973.

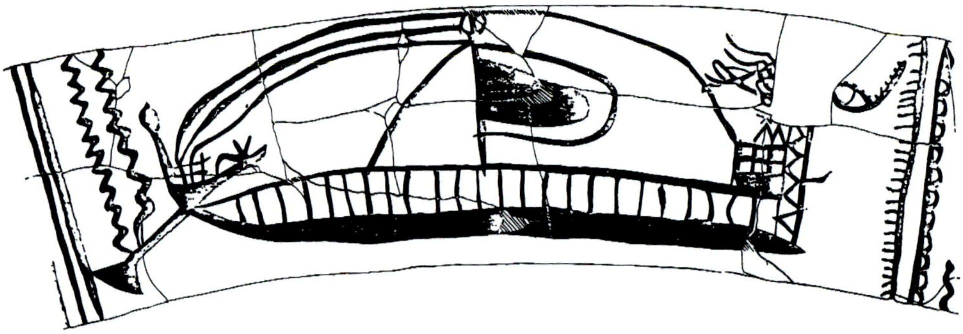

Figure 7. The ship depicted on the Late Helladic IIIC pyxis from the Tragana Tholos Tomb.

Figure 8. The ship depicted on the Cretan clay sarcophagus of Gazi.

Figure 9. Geometric hulls from Greek potteries.

reproduce some oars.[28] Nonetheless, Morrison and Williams[29] have argued, the restoration of the general shape of the boat that was proposed by Theochares based on this image[30] cannot be accepted, as it is not reliant on archaeological evidence. In addition, it is also not possible to confirm the presence of the steering oar.

The best-preserved depiction of a Mycenaean ship available to us dates from some centuries later, and comes from Messenia (Figure 7). Depicted on a Mycenaean pyxis from the Tragana Tholos Tomb dated to the Late Helladic III c, it shows a ship to the right, with a continuous line running from the top of the stern post to the end of the bow. Analysis of this image, especially when conducted in the light of other images of ships dating to the second half of the second millennium BC, like the one of the matt-painted Middle Helladic vase from Volos,[31] that of the stirrup vase from Asine dated to the Late Helladic IIIc,[32] the three found depicted on the fragments from Phylakopy dated to te Late Helladic III[33] or the one from Eleusis,[34] makes it possible to form a general idea of the kind of ships that were in use during the Mycenaean era between the sixteenth and eleventh centuries BC.[35] In this all of these depictions, it is possible to identify the presence of some sort of ram, or at least of a protrusion of the keel line ahead of the stem-post. The most of these images of Mycenaean ships show a mixed form of propulsion, with a single line of oars on each side, and what can be inferred as a squared sail on a mast, usually placed centre-hull. At the stern, a steering oar to drive the boat is identifiable. Despite only being rough sketches, the depictions available to us suggest the presence of two superstructures, one just over the gunwale line, at the bow and the other at the stern. A series of vertical lines traced along the side of the ship may mark the space allocated for the oarsmen.[36] Usually numbering 24, these lines would seem to indicate that there was space for twenty-five oarsmen on each side of the vessel, and this suggests a possible interpretation of these ships as the ancestors of the πεντηκοντέροι of the Geometric period.[37] However, a comparison of these line drawings with the clay models found at Mycene, Tanagra, Asine, and Phylacopi,[38] does not resolve the question as to whether these lines can be interpreted as a representation of the internal framing, a technical element that is typical of the sewn-building tradition,[39] and that is archaeologically attested in finds from the area dating back to at least the mid-second millennium BC.[40]

Similar decoration can be identified on the ships engraved on the internal surface of a pillar found in Dramesi[41] and dated to the 13th century BC,[42] as well as on a ship depicted on a Cretan

[28] Morrison, Williams 1968: 9.
[29] Morrison and Williams 1968: 9.
[30] Theochares 1958: 15.
[31] Morrison, Williams 1968: 9.
[32] Casson 1971: pl. 29.
[33] Morrison, Williams 1968: 10-11.
[34] Morrison, Williams 1968: 10.
[35] Morrison, Williams 1968: 7-11; Basch 1987: 140-49; Casson 1971: 30-32.
[36] Morrison, Williams 1968: 7-8.
[37] Basch 1987: 141-42.
[38] Basch 1987: 140-42
[39] On this topic, and on the possibility of internal hide framing on LBA Levantine Boats see Pulak 2003.
[40] Van de Moortel 2012.
[41] According to Basch Dramesi is 'a small town of Boeotia, not far from Aulis, from where the Achaean fleet moved to Troy' (Basch 1987: 143).
[42] Basch 1987: 143-44.

clay sarcophagus found at Gazi, about 6 km from Heraklion,[43] dated to 1200 BC (Figure 8). This latter item, in particular, includes many of the features typical of images from this period, such as a central mast, the two superstructures at bow and stern, a prolongment of the keel line, and vertical lines along the side of the ship. In addition, the presence of a square-sail, partially furled, appears to confirm that the central vertical line could be read as a main-mast, and that the vessel relied on mixed propulsion.

As we have seen, between 1600 and 1100 BC, the presence of several types of ship, all similar but nonetheless featuring some variation, seems to reflect the idea of the existence of 'several Mycenaean fleets [...] properties of different princes [...] of which the Homeric Catalogue of Ships may represents a reliable reflection'.[44] While it is, of course, possible that all these images reflect the situation at the time of the Trojan war, if we turn to a study of Homeric society more generally, we can clearly notice how, during the Geometric Period, the purely Greek images of ships appear to increase in number, which would seem to provide us with some important information regarding the evolution of shape of these vessels. The depictions of ships of the Geometric period found at Attica, although to an extent anticipated by the proto-geometric galleys of Crete,[45] thus mark a crucial development in the history of Greek shipbuilding.

From at least the first quarter of the eighth century BC, the Geometric hulls depicted on vases[46] appear to be more complex, presenting at least two rows of oarsmen, together with an intricate profile (Figure 9). The two ends differ: at the stern of the ship, the hull has a rounded shape, while at the prow, a projection of the keel line seems to suggest the presence of a possible spur, or of a ram. The stem-post is almost vertical, with an upper projection that turns back on itself towards the hull, just above the gunwale line. At the prow, a structure, maybe a forecastle, is also identifiable, together with a bridge-rail. The oarsmen sit on thwarts, with the oars fixed at a sort of rail-platform, which is reproduced just above the possible gunwale in a depiction that is usually interpreted as showing two possible decked portions. Above the platform, the two end-posts protrude upwards, and partially turn inwards, suggesting the presence of a parasemon at prow, and of an aplastron at stern.

All of these features can be considered as distinctive design elements of Greek shipbuilding technique. In some cases, such as with the aplastron, these features were carried over from the Bronze Age, as a number of both Minoan and Mycenaean ship images can testify.[47] Furthermore, and as has been demonstrated in a number of studies,[48] the iconography of Greek ships from the Geometric period onwards began to codify certain elements of ship design, including fixing forms and proportions for the ships. From this point onwards, Greek hulls are far more easily recognized in iconography thanks to the presence of the apotropaic eye at bow, the parasemon at stern, the upper projection at prow, and the protrusion ahead of

[43] Basch 1987: 146.
[44] Basch 1987: 156.
[45] Basch 1987: 179-81.
[46] Morrison, Williams 1968: 12-42; Gray 1974.
[47] Casson 1971: pl. 34-46.
[48] Morrison, Williams 1968; Casson 1971; Basch 1987; Pomey 1996; McGrail 2000

the keel line. This is also the case even when these vessels are depicted in a foreign context, such as an image found in Etruria,[49] for example, or similarly one identified in the Balkans.[50]

While study of the naval iconography from the Homeric period makes it possible to form an idea of the nautical dimension of Greek Culture at this time, as well as to tentatively identify this time frame as the possible cradle of Classical Greek maritime culture, if we turn to the archaeology of ships and wrecks from this period, it is clear that the archaeological record indicates a far more complex situation. Investigations from the 1970s onwards into several wooden hulls that were found around the coastline of the Mediterranean basin indicate a significant change to the wooden structures of Greek ships, particularly from a technical perspective, between eighth and sixth centuries BC. As Patrice Pomey has noted, structural analysis of wrecks up to now has tended to give particular emphasis to the contact between the Greek and the Levantine shipbuilding traditions, and the impact this would have had on the development of new technological solutions. With regards to hull construction, for example, a study of extant wrecks makes it possible to identify the shift from the typical Greek sewing technique,[51] which was used from at least the mid-second Millennium BC onward,[52] to the introduction of Phoenician mortise-and-tenon joining,[53] which appeared between the 5th and 4th century BC in connection with the introduction of the classical trireme. Direct evidence of this progressive hybridization of the Greek shipbuilding tradition can be found both in the western Mediterranean, as with the wrecks of Mazarròn 1 and 2 in Spain[54], the wreck of Golo in Corsica,[55] and that of Gela 1 in Sicily,[56] and in the eastern Mediterranean, such as that at Pabuç Burnu on Turkish coast.[57]

With regards to a study of ancient texts, an analysis of written sources in the light of iconography and the material remains of wrecks appears to confirm that the time between the Geometric and the Archaism was very much a transitional period, mainly characterised by a progressive growth of the naval presence of the Greeks and Phoenicians, throughout the Mediterranean. This very much supports the notion of a possible technological hybridization in shipbuilding. According to Thucydides[58] the very first presence of the Πελοποννήσιοι, 'Greeks of the Sea', in the west, particularly in Ἰταλίας, Italy, and in Σικελίας, Sicily, was linked to the use of the πεντηκοντόροις δ᾽ ἔτι καὶ πλοίοις μακροῖς , the 'ships of fifty oars and [of the] long merchant ships'. These older hull-types were then transformed in a later period by Ameinocles, the Corinthian shipwright who invented the new τριήρεις, the oared ships of the seventh century BC, 'which surely felt the effect of the colonization'.[59]

> πρῶτοι δὲ Κορίνθιοι λέγονται ἐγγύτατα τοῦ νῦν τρόπου
> μεταχειρίσαι τὰ περὶ τὰς ναῦς, καὶ τριήρεις ἐν
> Κορίνθῳ πρῶτον τῆς Ἑλλάδος ναυπηγηθῆναι.

49 Tiboni 2016.
50 Tiboni 2018.
51 Pomey, Kahanov 1984.
52 Van De Moortel 2012.
53 Pomey 2012.
54 Negueruela 2005.
55 Pomey 2009.
56 Benini 2012.
57 Polzer 2010.
58 Thucydides, *Peloponnesian War* I.12-14.
59 Pomey 1996: 138.

> φαίνεται δὲ καὶ Σαμίοις Ἀμεινοκλῆς Κορίνθιος
> ναυπηγὸς ναῦς ποιήσας τέσσαρας.
>
> It is said that the Corinthians were the first to approach
> the modern style of naval architecture,
> and that Corinth was the first place in Hellas where triremes were built.
> And we have Ameinocles, a Corinthian shipwright,
> making four ships for the Samians.[60]

A further confirmation of the use of the 'ships with fifty oars' during the earliest colonial journeys, particularly during the eighth century BC, comes from Herodotus:

> οἱ δὲ Φωκαιέες οὗτοι ναυτιλίῃσι μακρῇσι πρῶτοι Ἑλλήνων ἐχρήσαντο,
> καὶ τὸν τε Ἀδρίην καὶ τὴν Τυρσηνίην καὶ τὴν Ἰβηρίην
> καὶ τὸν Ταρτησσὸν οὗτοι εἰσὶ οἱ καταδέξαντες:
> ἐναυτίλλοντο δὲ οὐ στρογγύλῃσι νηυσὶ ἀλλὰ πεντηκοντέροισι
>
> These Phocaeans were the earliest of the Greeks to make long sea-voyages,
> and it was they who discovered the Adriatic Sea, and the Tyrrhenian, and Iberia,
> and Tartessus: not sailing in round freight-ships but in fifty-oared vessels.[61]

In this passage, Herodotus thus provides us with information about the ship-type that was in use during the first commercial and colonial explorations from Greece. At the same time, he informs us that during this period, which corresponds with the Middle Geometric,[62] there was evidently a close relationship between Greeks and the Phoenicians sailors,[63] particularly in the western part of the Mediterranean basin. We know, in fact, that the city of Ταρτησσὸν, 'Tartessos', and the Ἰβηρίην, 'Iberian Peninsula', were both under Phoenician influence from at least the tenth or ninth centuries BCE.[64] This notion of a close relationship between the Greeks and Phoenicians in the western Mediterranean finds support in the discovery of a fragment of an Euboean skyphos with birds at Huelva, in southern Spain,[65] usually dated to the Middle Geometric II,[66] as well as in the finds of several ceramic shreds of Greek origin in some of the earliest settlement layers at Carthage, and in Carthaginian burial contexts of the eighth century BC.[67]

The archaeology of wrecks, examination of images of ships, and analysis of texts together thus permit us to state that at the time of that Homer was working, Greek society and culture was very closely connected to the sea and to seafaring. It is hardly mere coincidence, then, that the *Iliad* and the *Odyssey*, which are effectively *sacred* texts, both had a strong naval dimension. It is with this understanding of the Homeric social and cultural framework in mind that we can

[60] Thucydides, *Peloponnesian War* I.13.
[61] Herodotus, *Histories* I.163.
[62] Guzzo 2011: 71.
[63] According to Sciortino and Krueger, we can also suppose the existence of 'joint ventures of Greek and Phoenicians sailors just at the beginning of the colonial adventure' (Sciortino, Krueger 2009: 345).
[64] Fantar 2004: 38-41.
[65] D'Agostino 1967: 29; Gras 1992: 38-41.
[66] Guzzo 2011: 45.
[67] Korou 2006: 92-96.

now turn to the Homeric texts, and endeavour to examine them from a naval-archaeological perspective.

Homer as a source for naval archaeology

As a number of scholars have stated,[68] the Homeric epics are an important primary source for our knowledge of ships in the Early Iron Age Mediterranean. In both the *Iliad* and the *Odyssey*, the author presents images of ships and seafaring, demonstrating clear knowledge of these topics.[69] However, Homer's descriptions do not simply provide us with general information about ships and the sea: vocabulary is used in a very precise fashion in these epic verses, meaning that when we read the poems, 'we are confronted with a system of nautical terminology, which seems surprisingly developed and closed', and that shows 'a real knowledge of the shipbuilding sector, the technical terminology, shared also with the audience'.[70] As such, for all that we may lack any detail about the structure of the ships from the time when Homer was working, if we extrapolate from what we know of the technical features of the ancient hulls, we can nonetheless turn to Homer's texts and identify particular elements about the building of vessels, since he often wrote as a real shipwright.

This understanding is emphasised most clearly when we turn, for example, to, a well-known passage from the *Odyssey*, which details the building of the boat that Odysseus used to leave Ogigia Island, the homeland of Calypso.[71] Here, the poem offers the following detail about ancient shipbuilding.

> εἴκοσι δ' ἔκβαλε πάντα, πελέκκησεν δ' ἄρα χαλκῷ,
> ξέσσε δ' ἐπισταμένως καὶ ἐπὶ στάθμην ἴθυνεν.
> τόφρα δ' ἔνεικε τέρετρα Καλυψώ, δῖα θεάων:
> τέτρηνεν δ' ἄρα πάντα καὶ ἥρμοσεν ἀλλήλοισιν,
> γόμφοισιν δ' ἄρα τήν γε καὶ ἁρμονίῃσιν ἄρασσεν.
> ὅσσον τίς τ' ἔδαφος νηὸς τορνώσεται ἀνὴρ
> φορτίδος εὐρείης, ἐὺ εἰδὼς τεκτοσυνάων,
> τόσσον ἔπ' εὐρεῖαν σχεδίην ποιήσατ' Ὀδυσσεύς.
> ἴκρια δὲ στήσας, ἀραρὼν θαμέσι σταμίνεσσι,
> ποίει: ἀτὰρ μακρῇσιν ἐπηγκενίδεσσι τελεύτα.
> ἐν δ' ἱστὸν ποίει καὶ ἐπίκριον ἄρμενον αὐτῷ:
> πρὸς δ' ἄρα πηδάλιον ποιήσατο, ὄφρ' ἰθύνοι.
> φράξε δέ μιν ῥίπεσσι διαμπερὲς οἰσυΐνῃσι
> κύματος εἶλαρ ἔμεν: πολλὴν δ' ἐπεχεύατο ὕλην.
>
> Twenty trees in all did he fell, and trimmed them with the axe;
> then he cunningly smoothed them all and made them straight to the line.
> Meanwhile Calypso, the beautiful goddess, brought him augers;
> and he bored all the pieces and fitted them to one another,
> and with pegs and morticings did he hammer it together.

[68] Morrison, Williams 1968: 43-69; Kurt 1979; Basch 1987: 157-58; Mc Grail 2001: 126-28.
[69] On the importance of Homer as a primary source for naval archaeology, see Kurt, 1979 and Mark, 2000.
[70] Kurt 1979: 219.
[71] Homer, *Odyssey* V. 244-257.

> Wide as a man well-skilled in carpentry marks out the curve of the hull of a freight-ship,
> broad of beam, even so wide did Odysseus make his raft.
> And he set up the deck-beams, bolting them
> to the close-set ribs, and laboured on;
> and he finished the raft with long gunwales.
> In it he set a mast and a yard-arm, fitted to it,
> and furthermore, made him a steering-oar, wherewith to steer.
> Then he fenced in the whole from stem to stern with willow withes
> to be a defence against the wave, and strewed much brush thereon.

In these verses, Homer in fact provides us with some interesting information about ancient Greek shipbuilding that would otherwise be lost to us due to the lack of any direct or material evidence.

Taking the craft as a starting point, we can see from verse 251, when describing the Bessel build by Odysseus, Homer did not use the term ναῦς or πλοῖον to indicate the vessel he used, but instead referred to it as to a σχεδία.[72] According to Casson, this term 'like its Latin synonym *ratis*, is frequently used in poetry in the sense of *boat*',[73] and we thus cannot refer to this particular boat as a raft. Further, as André Tchernia, has commented, the use of the term σχεδία was linked to Homer's need to introduce a particular kind of boat, 'a tub, a makeshift craft, no doubt big, as well done as a non-professional could do, but lacking, even if it was built in the same way, too many essential qualities for it to be called boat or ship'.[74] With regards to the vessel's cultural attribution, the analysis of the text[75] allows us to affirm that this σχεδία was assembled according to a purely Greek tradition, with the plan for the boat conceived around the creation of a shell, built first, and with the planks of the hull in fact sewn together to create the σχεδίης πολυδέσμου, 'sewn'[76] that was indicated by Zeus as the way for Odysseus to leave Calypso's homeland. From a technical point of view, this passage also informs us that Greek shipwrights would make use of a χαλκῷ 'copper axe', that they created the tetrahedral holes to the stitches by means of τέρετρα 'augers', and that the planks were then ἁρμονίῃσιν, 'fastened together', as is indeed the case on many of the wrecks of Greek origin that have been discovered in the Mediterranean.[77]

The meaning of many of the elements described by Homer in this passage, although presumably clearly understandable to the original audience, were for a long time lost, and have been recently been properly understood by modern scholars only in recent, mainly thanks to the results of naval archaeological investigation. As George F. Bass has argued, for instance,

> Odysseus's last task in building a boat was to 'spread over it a great deal of brushwood (πολλὴν δ' ἐπεχεύατο ὕλην). Its purpose was seldom understood by many modern

[72] Some verses before, Calypso said that Odysseus had to leave the island using a εὐρεῖαν σχεδίην, 'a broad craft' (Hom., *Odyssey* V, 163).
[73] Casson 1971: 217.
[74] Tchernia 2001: 630.
[75] This interpretation is supported, among the others, by Mark (2000) and Tchernia (2001: 625-6) contra Casson (1964).
[76] Homer, *Odyssey* V.33. The words can be literally translated '*tub with many flexible connections*'.
[77] Pomey, Kahanov, Rieth 2012.

> translators of Homer before the discovery of a ship which sank about the time of the Trojan War. Here an excavator from the University of Pennsylvania Museum cuts beneath the brushwood dunnage, with bark still preserved, which lined the hull of the Bronze Age ship near Cape Gelydonia, Turkey. Most of the vessel had been destroyed by shipworms, but fragmentary wooden members revealed that methods used in its construction were identical to those described by Homer.[78]

While it is quite obvious that a technical language can provide us with some information about some elements of construction, it is perhaps more surprising when 'some technical aspects can be deduced from the linguistic material'.[79] This in fact happens in several passages of Homer's epics, and gives us a precise idea of the impact of naval archaeology finds in the comprehension of the text. This can be seen, for instance, in the *Iliad* II.134-135:

> ἐννέα δὴ βεβάασι Διὸς μεγάλου ἐνιαυτοί,
> καὶ δὴ δοῦρα σέσηπε νεῶν καὶ σπάρτα λέλυνται:
>
> Already have nine years of great Zeus gone by,
> and lo, our ships' timbers are rotted, and the tackling loosened.

These lines clearly provide us with a small amount of information concerning both the naval situation at the beginning of the Homeric narration of the Trojan War, and the ships that were used by the Achaeans to reach the beach of Troy.

In verse 134 of the second book of the *Iliad*, we read that, at the beginning of the narrated events, all the δοῦρα νεῶν, 'ship's timber,' were σέσηπε, 'rotten', and that the σπάρτα, 'tackling', were έλυνται 'loosened'. However, if we focus more precisely on the choice of vocabulary used, we can in fact suggest that the author does not generally refers to the ship's 'timber', but more specifically to the wood that was used to build the hull: the term chosen, δοῦρα, corresponds with the same term used in the *Odyssey* V.243, when reference is made to the wood used by Odysseus to build his σχεδία:

> αὐτὰρ ὁ τάμνετο δοῦρα: θοῶς δέ οἱ ἤνυτο ἔργον
>
> but he fell to cutting timbers, and his work went forward apace

With regard to the σπάρτα, 'tackling', we can now, as a result of discoveries made in the last decades of the twentieth century and particularly those of the Archaic Greek sewn hulls of the Western Mediterranean,[80] translate this term with its proper meaning. It would appear that when he used this word, Homer was referring deliberately to the vegetal fibres that were used to create the lanyards with which the planks of the ships were sewn. These, he labelled έλυνται, 'loosened', as a reference to the ships' long abandonment on the beach.

These two verses, which would have been clearly understandable for the Homeric audience, make it clear that in this narrative epic, the besiegers reached the Trojan beach on board

[78] Bass 1972: 24.
[79] Kurt 1979: 219.
[80] Pomey 2012.

sewn ships some nine years before the beginning of the events narrated in the *Iliad*. Moreover, given that the ships are here described as lying abandoned on the strand, it would seem that the hulls have been out of water for around nine years, and neither used to fight nor sail, meaning that at the time Homer's narrative begins, they could not easily be refitted. As was demonstrated in 2013 when the *Gyptis*, a replica of a sixth-century BC Greek sewn boat was constructed based on the *Jules-Verne 9*,[81] such vessels took a significant amount of time to create, meaning that the rebuilding of the Achaean Fleet could not had been considered as an option. Based on the material remains of ship wrecks from this period, it seems not unreasonable to suggest that Homer, in the passage cited here, at the beginning of the *Iliad*, was outlining to his audience a situation in which the Trojan War needed to be ended because, with the decay of the fleet, neither surrender nor withdrawal were an option. And it seems that the Homeric audience could easily understand it.

The naval context of the Homeric narration of the last night of Troy

It is with this awareness of the background knowledge about shops and seafaring that both Homer and his audience would have brought to the narrative that we can turn to the single account by Homer of the last night of Tory, and examine whether he might not have been talking about a horse, but in fact something quite different. While the next chapter provides a detailed discussion of the description given in the *Odyssey* of the contrivance that was used by the Greeks to break the walls of Troy, it is my intention here to examine the broader context of the fall of Troy as it is recounted by Homer.

In terms of the location in which events are said to take place, Homer presents the episode of the Horse quite explicitly in the land of the Phaeacians, a people descended from the mythical king Ναυσίθοος 'Nausithoos', who was himself one of the sons of Poseidon. The king's name, comprising the terms Ναυσ, 'ship', and θοος, 'fast', clearly points to the connection between the Phaeacians and the ships, and this link is suggested further by the description of the princess Ναυσίκαα 'Nausicaa' — a name composed again of the element Ναυσ 'ship', together with καα 'famous' — of the city of the Phaeacians, and this settlement's harbour:

> αὐτὰρ ἐπὴν πόλιος ἐπιβήομεν, ἣν πέρι πύργος
> ὑψηλός, καλὸς δὲ λιμὴν ἑκάτερθε πόληος,
> λεπτὴ δ' εἰσίθμη: νῆες δ' ὁδὸν ἀμφιέλισσαι
> εἰρύαται: πᾶσιν γὰρ ἐπίστιόν ἐστιν ἑκάστῳ.
> ἔνθα δέ τέ σφ' ἀγορὴ καλὸν Ποσιδήιον ἀμφίς,
> ῥυτοῖσιν λάεσσι κατωρυχέεσσ' ἀραρυῖα.
> ἔνθα δὲ νηῶν ὅπλα μελαινάων ἀλέγουσι,
> πείσματα καὶ σπεῖρα, καὶ ἀποξύνουσιν ἐρετμά.
> οὐ γὰρ Φαιήκεσσι μέλει βιὸς οὐδὲ φαρέτρη,
> ἀλλ' ἱστοὶ καὶ ἐρετμὰ νεῶν καὶ νῆες ἐῗσαι,
> ᾗσιν ἀγαλλόμενοι πολιὴν περόωσι θάλασσαν.

> But when we are about to enter the city, around which runs a lofty wall,
> a fair harbour lies on either side of the city

[81] Pomey, Poveda 2015: 12-71.

> and the entrance is narrow, and curved ships are drawn up along the road,
> for they all have stations for their ships, each man one for himself.
> There, too, is their place of assembly about the fair temple of Poseidon,
> fitted with huge stones set deep in the earth.
> Here the men are busied with the tackle of their black ships,
> with cables and sails, and here they shape the thin oar-blades.
> For the Phaeacians care not for bow or quiver,
> but for masts and oars of ships, and for the shapely ships,
> rejoicing in which they cross over the grey sea.[82]

Similar refences in several other stanzas also seem to confirm the importance of naval activity to the Phaeacians, and these together combine to create a very particular narrative context for the events of the last night of Troy. I will here briefly offer some detail of the most interesting elements of the account.

At the beginning of the seventh book of the *Odyssey*, Athena Pallas is shown guiding Odysseus to the palace of the king Alcinous, on which route they walk among the Φαίηκες ναυσικλυτοὶ, 'Phaeacian's glorious sailors'.[83] Later on in this same book, Odysseus, during his sojourn with the Phaeacians, narrates tales of his journey to Arete and Alcinous[84], and he also describes the boats that were used to sail the sea from Troy. At first, he utilizes the terms νῆα θοὴν, 'fast ship'[85] and νεὸς ἀμφιελίσσης, 'ship rowed on both sides',[86] to identify the hulls on which he sailed the sea prior to the first occasion on which his vessel was wrecked. Thereafter, he utilizes the words σχεδίης, 'tub',[87] and σχεδίης πολυδέσμου, 'swen'[88] to refer to the vessel he constructed in order to leave Calypso's homeland. The precise use of such nautical terminology indicates that in this passage, Odysseus is aware that his hosts, the king and the queen of the Phaeacians, are people of knowledge, and he is able to speak to them in technical terms, in the way that one mariner might speak to another. Through Odysseus, however, Homer is effectively talking to his audience in the same way, assuming a degree of technical understanding and anticipating that even specific terminology will be understood.

In all three books of the *Odyssey* — books six to eight — that are set in the homeland of the Phaeacians, nautical descriptions and technical vocabulary are a recurrent feature. This is particularly true of the eighth book, in which this naval dimension is amplified, for example when the Phaeacians prepare the ship to bring Odysseus home, and during the games and the feasts that are held in his honour. As such, it seems unlikely to be a coincidence that during this celebration, Homer, through the words of the herald of the king, elects to narrate certain events of the Trojan War to the audience, and, through the figure of Odysseus, to introduce the Trojan Horse.[89]

[82] Homer, *Odyssey* VI.262-272.
[83] Homer, *Odyssey* VII.39.
[84] Homer, *Odyssey* VII.241-297.
[85] Homer, *Odyssey* VII.249.
[86] Homer, *Odyssey* VII.252.
[87] Homer, *Odyssey* VII.274.
[88] Homer, *Odyssey* VII.264. The words can be literally translated 'tub with many flexible connections'.
[89] Homer, *Odyssey* VIII.491-495.

> ἀλλ' ἄγε δὴ μετάβηθι καὶ ἵππου κόσμον ἄεισον
> δουρατέου, τὸν Ἐπειὸς ἐποίησεν σὺν Ἀθήνῃ,
> ὅν ποτ' ἐς ἀκρόπολιν δόλον ἤγαγε δῖος Ὀδυσσεὺς
> ἀνδρῶν ἐμπλήσας οἵ ῥ' Ἴλιον ἐξαλάπαξαν.
>
> But come now, change thy theme, and sing of the building of the horse of wood,
> which Epeius made with Athena's help,
> the horse which once Odysseus led up into the citadel as a thing of guile,
> when he had filled it with the men who sacked Ilios.

As will be discussed in more detail in the following chapters, this short passage is the main source — and indeed, the only narrative connected to the Homeric Epics — available to us that offers any detail about the contrivance used by the Achaeans to conquer Troy. While modern-day translators of the *Odyssey* invariably understand this as being the first actual description of the simulacre of a wooden horse, created with divine assistance, such an understanding has not always been accepted. Pausanias (110-180 AD), for example, in his *Description of Greece* (I.23.8) noted the following:

> ἵππος δὲ ὁ καλούμενος Δούριος ἀνάκειται χαλκοῦς. καὶ ὅτι μὲν τὸ ποίημα τὸ Ἐπειοῦ μηχάνημα ἦν ἐς διάλυσιν τοῦ τείχους, οἶδεν ὅστις μὴ πᾶσαν ἐπιφέρει τοῖς Φρυξὶν εὐήθειαν: λέγεται δὲ ἔς τε ἐκεῖνον τὸν ἵππον ὡς τῶν Ἑλλήνων ἔνδον ἔχοι τοὺς ἀρίστους, καὶ δὴ καὶ τοῦ χαλκοῦ τὸ σχῆμά ἐστι κατὰ ταῦτα:
>
> There is the horse called the Wooden Horse, set up in bronze. That the work of Epeius was a contrivance to make a breach in the Trojan wall is known to everybody who does not attribute utter silliness to the Phrygians. But legend says of that horse that it contained the most valiant of the Greeks, and the design of the bronze figure fits in well with this story.

Here, Pausanias expresses doubt as to the precise nature of the μηχάνημα, 'contrivance', and suggests that the decision to interpret Epeius' work as a giant statue of a horse must have been a direct consequence of the narrative entering into legend. This is particularly clear through his use of the word 'λέγεται', used in the sense of 'it is said that', or 'the legend says'. But, at the time that Pausanias was writing, in the second century AD, many centuries had already passed from the point at which Homer initially narrated this story, and Greek culture, in particular its naval practices, as well as socio-cultural traditions, had undergone a significant transition.

Nonetheless, as I will explain in more detail in the following chapters, thanks to new developments in the discipline of naval archaeology, and with an awareness of how familiar Homer and his audience must in fact have been with naval and maritime themes and terminology, it is now possible to suggest a solution to Pausanias's doubt. This seems to be find further support from the Byzantine author Johannes Lydus (490-560 AD) in his *De Mensibus*; here, the author discusses a sentence that, according to the *Analecta Alexandrina* of philologist

Augustus Meineke, in fact constitutes fragment CXX of a lost poem by the Greek poet and grammarian Euphorion of Calchis, born *c.* 275 BC. Lydus thus notes:[90]

> Περὶ τοῦ Δουρέιου ἵππου ὁ Εὐφορίων φεσί
> πλοῖον γενέσθαι τοῖς Ἑλλησιν ἵππον λεγόμενον.
>
> With regards to the wooden horse, Euphorion says
> it was a boat called horse by the Greeks.[91]

Intriguingly, if we focus more specifically on the vocabulary used by Lydus, it would seem that Euphorion in fact identified the contrivance used by the Achaeans not as being a simple boat, but in fact as a proper merchant-ship 'πλοῖον',[92] called horse 'ἵππον λεγόμενον', by the Greeks as 'τοῖς ''Ελλησιν'.

As I will go on to argue in the rest of this book, it is possible, thanks to new material finds from a maritime context, to identify the kind of ships that the 'Greek writers dubbed *hippoi* because of their figurehead'.[93] On the basis of our present knowledge in the fields of ancient shipbuilding, of navigation, and of maritime activities, we can now plausibly argue that in his narration of the events leading up to the Fall of Troy, Homer never in fact referred to a giant horse made from wood. The results of maritime archaeology, through the study of the images of ships, as well as of the texts pertaining to ships and navigation, and of the wrecks of ancient hulls, thus permit us to take a decisive step forward on a path first traced in the late nineteenth century by the scholar Cecil Torr. In his work, Torr proclaimed: 'in the legend of the taking of Troy through the stratagem of the Wooden Horse, there is perhaps a reminiscence of the capture of some seaport town by men concealed on board a ship, which had unwarily been admitted within the harbour'.[94] As I shall go on to demonstrate, the horse cited by Homer was indeed a ship.

---

[90] Johannes Lydus, *De Mensibus* IV.88.

[91] This is the translation by Andrew Eastburne for Roger Pearse in 2013 of John Lydus, *De Mensibus*, p. 240.

[92] The term πλοῖον indicates a merchant-ship specifically, and is not simply a generic term for ship. As we can see, for example, in Thucydides, the term πλοῖον is used separately to ναυσ: 'καὶ οἱ μὲν Ἀθηναῖοι τοῖς τε πλοίοις καὶ ταῖς ναυσὶ τούτῳ τῷ τρόπῳ ἐκλιπόντες τὸ χωρίον ἐς Παλλήνην διεκομίσθησαν:' 'In this way the place was evacuated by the Athenians, who went across in their merchant-boats and warships to Pallene' (Thucydides, *Peloponnesian War* IV.116.2).

[93] Casson 1994: 41.

[94] Torr, 1895: 114.

The Wooden Horse in Ancient Texts

Before introducing the study of the Homeric δουρατέος ἵππος from a naval point of view, I will try to examine the episode from its textual perspective as it permits to highlight some problems relating to the 'legend', often still present in the modern literature.

The Wooden Horse is one of the most famous episodes of the entire ancient narration of the Fall of Troy. Well-known by modern audience thanks to some later poems, paintings, and, most recently, films, the concept of the Trojan Horse has entered into our culture so deeply that, today, everyone has their own visual version of the *great horse* that was built by the Achaeans to conquer the city.

Most modern-day versions of the tale of the Trojan Horse appear to be based on a famous painting by Giandomenico Tiepolo, dated to the eighteenth century and now on display at the National Gallery in London. A product of the artist's own imagination, however, this work does not, in fact, reflect the narrative recorded in ancient texts: even though people today consider the Trojan Horse to be a crucial element in the Fall of Troy, very little of this narrative can be found in the ancient Greek poems. Initially circulating in oral tradition, before finally being written down at some point in the eighth century BC, when the Greek alphabet was first adopted,[1] the tradition of wooden horse being used by the Achaeans to conquer Troy formed an important component of the chronicles relating to the Trojan War. However, the Trojan Horse does not in fact feature in the two main poems of the Epic Cycle narrated or written by Homer, namely the *Iliad* and the *Odyssey*: the former work ends just before the destruction of Troy, while the latter poem, the story of the journey of Odysseus, in fact begins just after the defeat of the Trojans.

The majority of our information concerning the contrivance and building of the Trojan Horse comes from minor texts, and in particular the *Little Iliad* by Arktinos from Miletus, and the *Ilioupersis* attributed to Lesches from Mytilene, two epigones of Homer who probably produced their texts at some point between the seventh and sixth centuries BC.[2] During this period, at least four poets[3] seem to have sung of the events of the sack of Troy, possibly in order to 'complete' the narration of the Homeric texts:[4] alongside Arktinos and Lesches,[5] we can also identify works by Stesychorus and Ibykos, two authors from the Greek colonies of southern Italy.[6] These minor narrations, particularly the *Little Iliad* and the *Ilioupersis*, provided their ancient audience with accounts that expanded considerably on episodes that are only hinted at in the two main poems by Homer., Included among these are the key fights that

1 Rossi 1977; Hedreen 1995: 153; Reber 2007: 25.

2 Ingoglia 2000: 12-13; Scafoglio 2004: 291; Reber 2007: 25-28.

3 According to Ervin, we could probably add Sakadas of Argos to this list, even though we do not have enough information about this author (Ervin 1964: 51).

4 Scafoglio 2014a: 290

5 Griffin (1977: 39) dates these poems to the end of the seventh century BC, while Davies (1989) thinks that these poems must be dated later, to the sixth century BC. However, the presence of vases with figures referring to the *Little Iliad* by Lesches of Mytilene seems to suggest an early date (seventh century BC), at least for this poem — a point to which I shall return below.

6 Stesychorus was born in Sicily, at Himera (630 BC) and died in Catania (555 BC), while Ibikos was born in Southern Italy (Reggio Calabria) in the 6th century BC.

occurred during the Fall of Troy, as well the planning and construction of the wooden horse. Unfortunately, probably as a result of their somewhat minor role,[7] most of these later works are now lost; we have at our disposal only a few fragments of the original poems, usually preserved in later manuscripts, where they were rewritten, and reinterpreted some centuries after the original version was composed.

According to many scholars,[8] we can find the most complete version of these poems derived from Homer preserved in the *Crestomathy* by Proclus,[9] a text usually dated to the fifth century AD.[10] However, in this late works, the texts appear to be generated by a random overlap of multiple actions. Moreover, 'their characteristics allow us to exclude for them a literary ambition, [as] they were born to serve the *Iliad* and the *Odyssey*, to integrate their narration, and to provide them with a foreword and a sequel'.[11] Thus, the lack of a precise narrative in their drafting seems to led to a number of contradictions between these later narratives, as well as from the original Homeric epics from which they are derived.[12]

Known and circulated until at least the fifth century AD, the poems by Arktinos and Lesches appear to have formed the basis of other, later narratives concerning the Fall of Troy. These include works written by Publio Virgilio Marone, by Triphiodorus, and by Quintus of Smyrna, produced between the first century BC and the fourth century AD.[13] When it comes to exploring the ways in which the Trojan Horse is depicted, it is notable that the details continue to be expanded and reworked in these later texts. From only a few verses at the beginning of the so-called *nyktomachy* in both the *Little Iliad* and the *Ilioupersis*, the narrative has expanded to some 51 verses in Triphiodorus 51 (vv. 57–108) and 53 verses (vv. 104–156) in Book 12 of Quintus of Smyrna.

A crucial development in this respect is that while the summaries recorded by Proclus are derived from ancient Greek narratives that were themselves based on Homer,[14] the poems by Quintus and Triphiodorus were composed after the *Aeneid* by Vergil. In this latter poem, the long description of the fall of the city of Troy, and the key role played by the construction of the wooden horse, seem to be inspired by a direct knowledge of the ancient authors, and in particular the writings of Lesches and Arktinos.[15] However, in the *Aeneid*, this episode enters a new epic dimension — it is the genre of the Roman epic — and the description in the text is intended to serve as a celebration of the ancestors of Rome. Quintus and Triphiodorus, when they produced their poems on the Fall of Troy, might still have been working in the Greek tradition as epigones of Homer, but nonetheless they were aware of Virgil's work, and the existence of the *Aeneid* meant that they were obliged to put forward a far more detailed account of events, necessary to surpass the possible scepticism of the post-Vergilian audience.[16] Much

[7] Scafoglio 2014a: 299.
[8] Anderson 1997; Scafoglio 2004a: 2004b; Reber 2007.
[9] West 2003: 118-51.
[10] Scafoglio 2004b.
[11] Scafoglio 2004a: 309.
[12] Scafoglio 2004a: 291-308.
[13] Vian 1959: 88; Knauer 1964: 61; Miguélez-Cavero 2013: 56.
[14] Scafoglio 2014b.
[15] Austin 1959: 22-23; Ingoglia 2000: 11-12.
[16] '[Quintus and Triphiodorus needed to face] that unwieldy, inevitable problem confronting a Roman poet who wished to tell again the old story of Troy. The problem, that is, of convincing a sophisticated modern audience, the Vergil's audience, that their ancestors could have been taken in by so obvious stratagem' (Clausen, 2002: 60).

like in the writings of Arktinos and Lesches, then,[17] these later poets continued to expand and enrich their accounts of the Trojan Horse through the addition of many details that were not present in the original versions, but that were presumably intended 'to make the resulting statue not only credible but also seductive'.[18]

With the exception of some specific studies that have focused on how the differing narrative accounts of the Trojan Horse have impacted upon Greek art,[19] most scholarly studies emphasise the impact made by the *Aeneid* for the diffusion of the Trojan Horse in classical culture.[20] It can hardly be seen as coincidental that, from the first century BC onward, accounts concerning the horse began to include new details, nor that the texts by Triphiodorus and Quintus proved so rich in hitherto unmentioned detail.

With an understanding of this historiographical development in mind when studying the ancient iconography of the episode, it is thus necessary return to the earliest accounts by Homer if we want to explore the first traditions concerning the wooden horse. We need to find the correct approach to the Homeric texts, and being by stripping back the weight of later tradition and narrative development.

The original version of the δουρατέος ἵππος of Troy: Homer

According to the chronology of both the so-called Epic-Cycle and the late epigones,[21] the sole source we have at our disposal when we refer to the *original version* of what Homer narrated about the Trojan War appears to be Homer himself. More precisely, with regards to the episode of the Wooden Horse of Troy, the main text that we have to take into account is that of the *Odyssey*, the second epic poem by Homer, which was first narrated orally and then written down, around the eighth century BC, as discussed above. Even though the use of a wooden horse as a supposed weapon of war represents the main episode of the last night of Troy and its siege, it is notable that this description does not feature in the *Iliad*, where there is in fact no reference at all to the use of a wooden horse. Indeed, the so-called *Wooden Horse of Troy* only appears in the *Odyssey*.

According to the Homeric text, the Trojan Horse appears first in the fourth book, when Telemachus, the son of Odysseus, reaches the court of King Menelaus in Sparta. Here, while remembering Odysseus and the Trojan War, Menelaus refers to the Horse for the first time:[22]

> οἷον καὶ τόδ' ἔρεξε καὶ ἔτλη καρτερὸς ἀνὴρ
> ἵππῳ ἔνι ξεστῷ, ἵν' ἐνήμεθα πάντες ἄριστοι
> Ἀργείων Τρώεσσι φόνον καὶ κῆρα φέροντες.

[17] Scafoglio 2014a: 299-309.
[18] Miguélez-Cavero 2013: 77.
[19] Anderson 1997, Lowenstam 1997.
[20] Austin 1959, Sparkes 1971, Sadurska 1986, Fuchs 2007.
[21] Davies 1969, Griffin, 1997, Scafoglio 2004a, Miguelez-Cavero 2013.
[22] Homer, *Odyssey* IV. 271-273.

What a thing was this, too, which that mighty man wrought,
endured in the carved horse, wherein all we chiefs of the Argives
were sitting, bearing the Trojans death and fate![23]

In this passage, Menelaus adds that Helen reaches the Horse and:[24]

τρὶς δὲ περίστειξας κοῖλον λόχον ἀμφαφόωσα,
ἐκ δ' ὀνομακλήδην Δαναῶν ὀνόμαζες ἀρίστους,
πάντων Ἀργείων φωνὴν ἴσκουσ' ἀλόχοισιν.
αὐτὰρ ἐγὼ καὶ Τυδεΐδης καὶ δῖος Ὀδυσσεὺς
ἥμενοι ἐν μέσσοισιν ἀκούσαμεν ὡς ἐβόησας.
νῶι μὲν ἀμφοτέρω μενεήναμεν ὁρμηθέντε
ἢ ἐξελθέμεναι, ἢ ἔνδοθεν αἶψ' ὑπακοῦσαι:
ἀλλ' Ὀδυσεὺς κατέρυκε καὶ ἔσχεθεν ἱεμένω περ.
ἔνθ' ἄλλοι μὲν πάντες ἀκὴν ἔσαν υἷες Ἀχαιῶν,
Ἄντικλος δὲ σέ γ' οἶος ἀμείψασθαι ἐπέεσσιν
ἤθελεν. ἀλλ' Ὀδυσεὺς ἐπὶ μάστακα χερσὶ πίεζεν
νωλεμέως κρατερῇσι, σάωσε δὲ πάντας Ἀχαιούς:
τόφρα δ' ἔχ', ὄφρα σε νόσφιν ἀπήγαγε Παλλὰς Ἀθήνη.

Thrice didst thou go about the hollow ambush,
trying it with thy touch, and thou didst name aloud
the chieftains of the Danaans by their names,
likening thy voice to the voices of the wives of all the Argives.
Now I, and the son of Tydeus, and goodly Odysseus sat there in the midst
and heard thou didst call, and we two were eager to rise up
and come forth, or else to answer straightway from within,
but Odysseus held us back and stayed us, despite our eagerness.
Then all the other sons of the Achaeans held their peace,
but Anticlus alone was fain to speak and answer thee;
but Odysseus firmly closed his mouth with strong hands, and saved
all the Achaeans, and held him thus until Pallas Athena led thee away

In these verses, Homer introduces the presumed horse when it is already inside the wall, with the heroes hidden inside, waiting for night-time in order to exit and open the door of the city to their comrades, who wait on their ships not far from the coast of Troy. From a structural point of view, the only things we can argue is that the horse was *carved*, big enough to hide *all the chiefs of the Argives*, that the heroes within were sitting, that they could clearly hear what was going on outside, and that they could easily leave the horse when required. We know also that Athena Pallas was protecting the war-machine.

In the eighth book of the Odyssey, once again, Homer introduces the presumed wooden horse by narrating the events of the last night of Troy. In contrast to the description attributed to Menelaus, in this case, it is the Phaeacian Demodocus, a herald of the court with no direct

[23] *Homer. The Odyssey with an English Translation* by A.T. Murray, Ph.D. in two volumes. Cambridge, MA., Harvard University Press; London, William Heinemann, Ltd. 1919.
[24] Homer, *Odyssey* IV.277-289.

knowledge of what happened at Troy, who is asked to narrate the events concerning the horse and the entry into Troy. Homer, however, perhaps to substantiate this description, then has Odysseus affirm this description:[25]

> Δημόδοκ', ἔξοχα δή σε βροτῶν αἰνίζομ' ἁπάντων.
> ἢ σέ γε μοῦσ' ἐδίδαξε, Διὸς πάϊς, ἢ σέ γ' Ἀπόλλων:
> λίην γὰρ κατὰ κόσμον Ἀχαιῶν οἶτον ἀείδεις,
> ὅσσ' ἔρξαν τ' ἔπαθόν τε καὶ ὅσσ' ἐμόγησαν Ἀχαιοί,
> ὥς τέ που ἢ αὐτὸς παρεὼν ἢ ἄλλου ἀκούσας.
>
> Demodocus, verily above all mortal men do I praise thee,
> whether it was the Muse, the daughter of Zeus, that taught thee, or Apollo.
> For well and truly dost thou sing of the fate of the Achaeans,
> all that they wrought and suffered, and all the toils they endured,
> as though haply thou hadst thyself been present, or hadst heard the tale from another

Through these words, attributed to Odysseus, Homer thus invites his audience to believe in what the Phaeacian herald says about the *horse* and the end of Troy. Concerning the *horse* itself, moreover, the intervention by Odysseus goes somewhat further. In the following verses, the hero states:[26]

> ἀλλ' ἄγε δὴ μετάβηθι καὶ ἵππου κόσμον ἄεισον
> δουρατέου, τὸν Ἐπειὸς ἐποίησεν σὺν Ἀθήνῃ,
> ὅν ποτ' ἐς ἀκρόπολιν δόλον ἤγαγε δῖος Ὀδυσσεὺς
> ἀνδρῶν ἐμπλήσας οἵ ῥ' Ἴλιον ἐξαλάπαξαν.
>
> But come now, change thy theme, and sing of the building
> of the horse of wood, which Epeius made with Athena's help,
> the horse which once Odysseus led up into the citadel as a thing of guile,
> when he had filled it with the men who sacked Ilios.

In these few lines, Homer provides us with different elements pertaining to the *wooden horse*. First, Epeius built the *horse*; Athena helped Epeius in building it; Odysseus led the crew of the *horse*; finally, the *horse* was used as a thing of guile.

A few verses later, Homer notes:[27]

> τοὶ δ' ἤδη ἀγακλυτὸν ἀμφ' Ὀδυσῆα
> ἥατ' ἐνὶ Τρώων ἀγορῇ κεκαλυμμένοι ἵππῳ:
> αὐτοὶ γάρ μιν Τρῶες ἐς ἀκρόπολιν ἐρύσαντο.
> ὣς ὁ μὲν ἑστήκει, τοὶ δ' ἄκριτα πόλλ' ἀγόρευον
> ἥμενοι ἀμφ' αὐτόν: τρίχα δέ σφισιν ἥνδανε βουλή,
> ἠὲ διαπλῆξαι κοῖλον δόρυ νηλέι χαλκῷ,

[25] Homer, *Odyssey* VIII.487-491.
[26] Homer, *Odyssey* VIII.492-495.
[27] Homer, *Odyssey* IV.502-507.

while those others led by glorious Odysseus
were now sitting in the place of assembly of the Trojans, hidden in the horse;
for the Trojans had themselves dragged it to the citadel.
So there it stood, while the people talked long as they sat about it,
and could form no resolve. Nay, in three ways did counsel find favour in their minds:
either to crave the hollow timber with the pitiless bronze.

These verses once again make it clear that Odysseus was the captain of those hidden in the horse and that the horse entered into the citadel dragged by the Trojans.

In another part of the poem, Homer confirms the information he has already given elsewhere concerning the building of the wooden horse. In the eleventh book of the *Odyssey*, in fact, while talking to the soul of Achilles, Odysseus states:[28]

αὐτὰρ ὅτ᾽ εἰς ἵππον κατεβαίνομεν, ὃν κάμ᾽ Ἐπειός,
Ἀργείων οἱ ἄριστοι, ἐμοὶ δ᾽ ἐπὶ πάντα τέταλτο,
ἠμὲν ἀνακλῖναι πυκινὸν λόχον ἠδ᾽ ἐπιθεῖναι,
ἔνθ᾽ ἄλλοι Δαναῶν ἡγήτορες ἠδὲ μέδοντες
δάκρυά τ᾽ ὠμόργνυντο τρέμον θ᾽ ὑπὸ γυῖα ἑκάστου:
κεῖνον δ᾽ οὔ ποτε πάμπαν ἐγὼν ἴδον ὀφθαλμοῖσιν
οὔτ᾽ ὠχρήσαντα χρόα κάλλιμον οὔτε παρειῶν
δάκρυ ὀμορξάμενον: ὁ δέ γε μάλα πόλλ᾽ ἱκέτευεν
ἱππόθεν ἐξέμεναι, ξίφεος δ᾽ ἐπεμαίετο κώπην
καὶ δόρυ χαλκοβαρές, κακὰ δὲ Τρώεσσι μενοίνα.

And again, when we, the best of the Argives,
were about to go down into the horse which Epeius made,
and the command of all was laid upon me,
both to open and to close the door of our stout-built ambush,
then the other leaders and counsellors of the Danaans
would wipe away tears from their eyes, and each man's limbs shook beneath him,
but never did my eyes see his fair face grow pale at all,
nor see him wiping tears from his cheeks;
but he earnestly besought me to let him go forth from the horse,
and kept handling his sword-hilt and his spear heavy with bronze,
and was eager to work harm to the Trojans.

In these few words, Odysseus informs us that the war-machine was built by Epeius, that he was the commander of this expedition and that he was expected to open and close the door of the machine.

Even though we clearly lack any detail about its structure or particular features, the verses cited here clearly provide us with certain information about the *wooden horse of Troy*. Moreover, this information must have been easily comprehensible for the Homeric audience for whom this epic was composed. Clearly, the details here sufficed, and there was no need for

[28] Homer, *Odyssey* XI.523-532.

further specific detail. It would not seem to be coincidence that it was some centuries before other authors (Arktinos, Lesches, Vergil, Quintus of Smyrna or Triphiodorus) felt the need to provide clearer and more precise descriptions outlining the figure of the horse.[29] However, if we look more closely at the descriptions given here, it might seem that in their attempt to make the construction of the so-called Trojan Horse more *convincing,*[30] more *credible, but also seductive,*[31] these later authors were actually guilty of a major misinterpretation of the text. As indirect witnesses to the story, it is not impossible that they tried to describe a fact that they did not know directly, and that was established through an unsupported deductive process, thus handing down a 'fact-not-true'.[32] More than one element of Homer's works has been open to interpretation[33], and in the case of the 'horse', it is by no means impossible that the words written by Homer were in fact imbued with a more precise meaning than they would in fact appear to have to a non-maritime audience.

The first element that we notice is that in all the passages referring to the so-called *horse*, the word ἵππος is always alone, or with adjectives that specify its structural features, such as δουρατέους. However, none of these adjectives ever specify any detail about the dimensions of the 'horse', perhaps suggesting that this might already be clear to the audience.[34] A second point to consider is that in one case,[35] the ἵππῳ ('horse') is said to be ξεστῷ ('carved'), while in a second description[36] the ἵππου ('horse') is δουρατέου ('made of wood').

From a linguistic point of view, while ἵππος might be translated as 'horse', the word δουρατέου, usually translated with 'wooden/made of wood', is not directly linked to the word δόρυ, which indicates the tree, but rather with the word δούρατα. This latter term, as demonstrated by Homer himself, should be translated as 'planks', in the naval sense of 'the planks of the bulwark of a hull'. In the fifth book of the *Odyssey*, in fact, the word δούρατα is first used by Calypsos when describing how to connect the planks of the hull of the raft.[37] Later, the same term is used twice to indicate the planks (δούρατα) of the destroyed raft,[38] and then to describe the single plank (δούρατι) that Odysseus uses to float in the rough sea.[39] Further, in the *Iliad* it is used to indicate the planks of the ships used to build a sort of palisade/wall to protect the ships on the beach.[40] The word ξεστῷ, which is usually translated with 'carved', derives from the verb ξέω, which means 'to smooth' as well as 'to carve'. In the fifth book of the Odyssey,

[29] Anderson 1997.
[30] Clausen 2002: 60.
[31] Miguélez-Cavero 2013: 77.
[32] 'Between the involuntary mistake and the intentional fake there is the "fact-not-true", that is furnished by a witness without a precise reason or a deceptive intent. It could happen that an author, just to demonstrate his own erudition (that means for a misunderstood and superficial ambition to complete a story), speaks about a fact he does not know, reconstructing it with an unsupported deductive process' (Scafoglio 2004a: 301).
[33] Other debates in this field concern, for example, about the correct identification of the feature of Odysseus' raft as described in *Odyssey* V, 228-277 (Casson 1956, Mark 2000, Janni 1996), or the identification of the Sewn Greek Boats on the base of Homer's *Iliad* II, 135.
[34] As we will see later, the additions of the dimensions are some of the first expansions to be added by Lesches, Arktinos, and Vergil.
[35] Homer, *Odyssey* IV.272.
[36] Homer, *Odyssey* IV.492-493.
[37] Homer, *Odyssey* V.162.
[38] Homer, *Odyssey* V.370.
[39] Homer, *Odyssey* V.371.
[40] Homer, *Iliad* VII. As we will see in the next chapter, the word δουρατέου will be changed into δουρέου in some laters iconographies. This is not due to a linguistic evolution, as the two words coexist with similar but different meanings in Greek texts at least until the 6th century AD.

when Homer describes what Odysseus did to prepare the planks for his raft, he again uses the verb ξέσσε,[41] the past of ξέω, when describing how the hero transforms the δούρα('trees') into the δούρατα ('planks') of his raft.

As we can see by reading the passages listed above, in order to avoid the repetition of the word ἵππος, Homer made use of some synonyms, such as κοῖλον λόχον 'concave hideout',[42] κοῖλον δόρυ 'concave wood',[43] πυκινὸν λόχον 'strong hideout'.[44] As for the word κοῖλον, usually translated into 'concave', in Homer's works, it is most often associated with the idea of the ἵππος to indicate its inner part. In more descriptive details, Homer uses this word in association with the terms δόρυ ('wood/tree) and λόχον ('hiding place'), metaphoric terms used to describe this machine of war. However, in ancient Greek texts, particularly when referring to the maritime world, the word is often used to indicate the hold of the ship, both in association with the term ναῦς ('ship')[45] or alone.[46] Even the word δόρυ is often used to define a ship when used in a metaphorical sense, both in association with the word ναῦς, as seen in different parts of the Odyssey, or on its own.[47]

The terms used by Homer to describe the actions that involved the horse also refer to the naval sphere. When describing how the ἵππος has entered the city, it is notable that the author employs the verb ἐρύσαντο,[48] the past of a verb that is most often translated into English as 'dragged'. However, Homer makes use of this verb in a number of verses in both the *Odyssey*, and the *Iliad*, in a far more specific sense, to indicate the launching and hauling of ships[49].

Arguably then, what we can see in a close reading of the texts, is that Homer often makes use of words that have a particular maritime connotation in connection to the so-called 'Trojan Horse'. Indeed, there appears to be a strong link between the 'horse' and the maritime world, and the terminology employed by Homer would in fact fit better if he were talking about a ship, with a stout-built hull made of planks and a cargo-hold, rather than the statue of a horse. With this awareness in mind, it is therefore useful to focus more closely on the word ἵππος.

As I will explore in more detail in the next chapter, several studies in naval archaeology[50] confirm that in ancient Greece the word ἵππος was in use to indicate a particular class of ship. This was a boat of Levantine design and origin, but that could be found throughout the Mediterranean world during the first half of the first millennium BC. According to the Greek historian Strabo, active between the end of the 1st century BC and the first quarter of the 1st century AD, in fact, at least until the second century BC, seamen from Cadiz, a Phoenician colony in southern Spain, used to sail on vessels that they 'called horses (ἵππος), from the figures of that animal borne on the prow, and in which they went out fishing around Maurusia,

[41] Homer, *Odyssey* V.245.
[42] Homer, *Odyssey* IV.277.
[43] Homer, *Odyssey* IV.507.
[44] Homer, *Odyssey* XI.525.
[45] Herodotus, *Histories* VIII. 199; Xenophon, *Hellenica* I.6.19; Demosthenes, *Letters* 883.
[46] Theocritus, *Idyllis* 22.12; Athaeneus, *fragment* 206, Appian, *The Civil Wars* V. In this latter example, we find the use of the plural τα κοῖλα for 'ships'.
[47] Sophocles, *Thrachiniae*; Euphorion, *Andromachas* 793. In this last example, the word δόρυ is used to define the Argo Ship.
[48] Homer, *Odyssey* V.371.
[49] Homer, *Iliad* IV.248; XIV.30; XIV.75; XVIII.69; *Odyssey* IV.666, IV.780; X.403; XI.2.
[50] Casson 1971: 65-68; Johnstone 1989: 83-85.

as far as the Lixus'.[51] Not knowing the name with which the Levantine peoples themselves used to identify their ἵππος, the oldest reference we can find for this particular class of ship in fact comes from Homer, namely the *Odyssey*.[52] Speaking of the ships that were used by Telemachus to sail the sea in search of his father, Penelope notes that those ships, which we know as merchantmen used by non-Greek people to trade metal, 'αἵ θ'ἁλὸς ἵπποι ἀνδράσι γίγνονται' ('are for the men the horses (ἵπποι) of the sea').[53] Once again, then, it would seem that analysis of the Homeric texts enables us to posit a direct link between the suggestion of a wooden horse and the ancient naval world. Moreover, there is more than one reason to suggest that we translate δουρατέος ἵππος as 'ship made of planks' rather than 'wooden horse'. However, before I go on to examine the naval dimensions of this argument in further detail, I would first like to pause and turn to the characters who were involved in the construction and use of the war machine that was taken into Troy.

Even though the creation of the Trojan Horse is widely remembered today as a deception that was ordered by Odysseus, a return to the texts shows Homer recording that the ἵππος was built by Epeius, with divine help from Athena.[54] Epeius himself does not appear to have been one of the most main actors in the history of the Trojan War.[55] According to Greek mythology,[56] Epeius was the son of Panopeius, who may well have arrived in Troy onboard one of the ships led by Nestor.[57] Throughout the whole siege of Troy, and even before to the final episode of the ἵππος, Epeius is in fact only mentioned twice, both times in connection to the games held in honour of Patroclus, when he is said to participate in both a boxing match[58] and in a discus-throwing competition.[59] On his journey back from Troy, Epeius is said to have sailed to Southern Italy and landed in the Gulf of Taranto, where he founded the colony of Metapontum, or Lagaria, in the place in which he devoted to Athena the tools that he used for the construction of the ἵππος.[60] With the exception of this dedication to Athena, however, we find no other reference in our textual sources, from Homer onwards, to show that Epeius had any specific ability as a blacksmith, carpenter, or shipwright. Indeed, Homer makes it very clear that he was able to build the ἵππος because he had Athena's help.[61]

---

[51] Strabo, *Geography* II.3-4

[52] Tiboni 2016: 98-99.

[53] Homer, *Odyssey* IV.708-709. We know that during the centuries, the metaphoric use of the term *horse* to indicate the ship will be quite common. As well pointed out, among the others, by Cecil Torr '*Ships of any sort could be described in metaphor as horses*', and we can also argue that '*The winged horse Pegasus may represent a ship with oars*' (Torr, 1895: 114). However, we cannot ignore that in all these metaphors the term *horse* substitutes the word *ship*. On the other hand, in these verses Homer underlined the fact that the ships of Menthes, king of the Tsaphian, were known as 'the horses of the sea'. Being merchant ships they cannot be oared, nor they could represent 'fast hulls', like it is intended in the metaphoric use of the word *horse* to indicate the *ships* (West 2007: 82-119).

[54] Homer, *Odyssey* VIII.493; XI.524.

[55] The Epeius who features in the works by Homer does not seem to be the one depicted by Pausanias: 'all agree that Endymion begat Paeon, Epeius, Aetolus, and also a daughter Eurycyda. Endymion set his sons to run a race at Olympia for the throne; Epeius won, and obtained the kingdom, and his subjects were then named Epeans for the first time.' (Pausanias, *Description of Greece* V.1.4).

[56] Grimal 1990: 212

[57] His link with Nestor seems to be connected to the journey back from Troy rather than to the beginning of the expedition. Homer does not indicate Epeius among the chief of the Argives in the Catalogue of Ships of the *Iliad*, while, according to Vergil, he was one of the Achaeans hidden in the ἵππος (Vergil, *Aeneid* II.264).

[58] Homer, *Iliad* XXIII.665-ff.

[59] Homer, *Iliad* XXIII.839-840.

[60] Grimal 1990: 212.

[61] Homer, *Odyssey* VIII.493.

In the *Odyssey*, Homer attests to the existence of a close relationship between Athena and the ἵππος twice: firstly, when the goddess helps Epeius in its construction,[62] and secondly, when she leads Helen away from the ἵππος while it stands in the citadel with the Argives on-board.[63] As far as Athena Pallas' involvement in the Trojan War goes, Homer's narratives suggest that the deity is seen to fight on for both sides on occasion: as the protector of the Argive, and particularly of Odysseus, both the *Iliad* and the *Odyssey* suggests that she is of help to Odysseus and his comrades. On the other hand, because the temple on the top of the citadel of Troy is devoted to Pallas – that is, to Athena Pallas – the goddess is often appears alongside the Trojans in the events narrated by the *Iliad*.[64]

Notably, in the *Odyssey*, Pallas Athena often appears in events linked to the construction and use of ships and boats. Included among these episodes are her invitation to Telemachus to embark on the ἵπποι of the Taphians;[65] her persuasion of Zeus to send his messenger to Calypso to make Odysseus build his raft;[66] and her involvement in convincing the Phaeacians to provide Odysseus with a ship for his journey back.[67] For the Greeks, Athena was the protector of the shipwrights, and this characteristic is usually linked to the construction of the Argo ship. According to Apollonius of Rhodes, in fact 'Argo built his ship with Athena's help',[68] using a beam of the Dodona oak for the keel[69] and smoothing the planks (δούρατα) with a bronze axe.[70] Written in the third century BC, this depiction of the construction of the Argo ship, preserved in Apollonius of Rhodes' *Argonautica*, shares a number of common elements with the construction of the ἵππος. Not only do both descriptions reference the presence of δούρατα, but the actors involved are also similar[71], the building of the ships benefits from divine support and as will be discussed below the use of different species of wood and the structures created also have significant similarities.

Structural elements of the δουρατέος ἵππος of Troy: Vergil

Even though the events narrated by Homer and by later authors such as Lesches and Arktinos date to some six centuries earlier than Vergil's *Aeneid*, our most detailed information about the technical structure of the ἵππος nonetheless comes from this latter poem, which is based on their direct knowledge. Written on behalf of the Emperor Augustus, mainly as a way of recording a noble ancestry for a new ruling dynasty, this epic give us some interesting information about the construction and the use of the ἵππος. Inspired by a direct knowledge of Arktinos' and Lesches' poems,[72] but free from the conditioning elements that affected the

---

[62] Homer, *Odyssey* VIII.493.
[63] Homer, *Odyssey* IV.289.
[64] According to ancient mythology (Grimal 1990: 471-73), Pallas was initially the name of a friend of Athena who died while playing with the goddess. After her death, Athena decided to adopt her qualities and characteristics, thus becoming the protector of the craftsmen and of the shipwright.
[65] Homer, *Odyssey* I.105-318.
[66] Homer, *Odyssey* V.5-20.
[67] Homer, *Odyssey* VIII.8 -23.
[68] Apollonius of Rhodes, *Argonautica* I.18-9; I.111-112.
[69] Apollonius of Rhodes, *Argonautica* I.526-527; III.580-583.
[70] Apollonius of Rhodes, *Argonautica* II.1187-1188.
[71] As the protector of shipwrights, Athena in both cases inspires and participates in the construction of the hulls, as well as suggesting the correct use of tools and raw materials. In the Ficoroni bronze cista we can see Athena helping Argo in building the ships. As we will see in the next chapters, this iconography recalls that of Athena working on the head of the horse depicted in a red-figure Kylix now at the National Archaeological Museum in Florence.
[72] Austin 1959: 22-3.

works of late Homeric epigones like Triphiodorus or Quintus of Smyrna,[73] Vergil was able to produce a description of the *equus ligneus* in the second Book of the Aeneid that is of great interest to the topic at hand.[74]

In his text, Vergil opens the narration of the events of the last night of Troy with the description of the *equus* made by Aeneas:[75]

> Danaum tot iam labentibus annis
> instar montis equum divina Palladis arte
> aedificant, sectaque intexunt abiete costas;
> votum pro reditu simulant; ea fama vagatur.
>
> Wearied of the war,
> and by ill-fortune crushed, year after year,
> the Kings of Greece, by Pallas' skill divine,
> build a huge horse, a thing of mountain size,
> with timbered ribs of fir. This is said.

In these few lines, the Latin author provides a lot of detail. First of all, as is made clear through the phrase *ea fama vagatur* ('this is said'), the author shows that Aeneas is referring to something that he knows well, but not deeply. This could, arguably, be understood as a reflection of Vergil's own position, as one who was familiar with events thanks to older poems, but who of course had never viewed anything as a direct witness.

Concerning the ἵππος, the first information that we are given here is the general dimension of the *equus ligneus*, which is said to have been built *instar monist* ('big as a mountain'). As we have seen above, Homer never mentioned the dimensions of the ἵππος, thus we can suppose that Vergil achieved this information through the reading of one of the poems by Arktinos or Lesches.[76] Nonetheless, in accordance with Homer, the Latin poet informs us that the *equus* was built following *divina Palladis arte* ('divine Pallas' skill'), thus confirming that the deity involved in this project was none other than the protector of shipwrights. However, contrary to Homer's report in the *Odyssey*, Vergil attributes the construction of the ἵππος to the 'Greeks'.

When describing the building of the *equus*, Vergil affirms that the builders use *secta abiete* ('planks of fir') to cover the sides. The term *costas*, usually translated into ribs, means in fact something quite different here. As we can see from elsewhere in the *Aeneid*, Vergil himself uses this term not to identify the ribs, but to indicate the sides of an object (*costis undantis aeni*).[77] Notably, we find this same term in texts written by Pliny, the admiral of the Roman Imperial fleet at Miseno, who died at Herculaneum in 79 AD, where is appears both in association with *navis* (*costas navium*) or alone (*costas*) to indicate the two bulwarks of the ancient hulls.[78]

[73] Clausen 2002: 60; Miguélez-Cavero 2013: 77.
[74] We cannot ignore the problem of the 'fact-not-true' as defined by Scafoglio (2014a: 301) see note 7.
[75] Vergil, *Aeneid* II.14-20.
[76] Austin 1959
[77] Vergil, *Aeneid* VII.463.
[78] Calonghi 1950: 691.

This link between Vergil's depiction of the *equus* and terminology from the naval sphere is further reinforced by similar terminology that appears in the 1st century BC in the *Carmina* by Catullus, in this case dedicated to the building of the Argo Ship:[79]

> Pallas levi fecit volitantem flamine currum,
> Pinea coniungens inflexae texta carinae,

> Pallas built for them a machine that flew at the first wind,
> She fixed the planks of pine to the sides of the hull.

In these lines, which predate and were probably known by Vergil[80] we find several elements in common with the *Aeneid*. Vergil goes on to recount that Pallas acts as ship-builder of the *equus*, the ἵππος, that the wood used to build the sides of the ships is conifer, and the planks of the hull are *texta*, like those of the ἵππος are *intexta*.

Given Vergil's description, it would appear that he, at least, possibly through a direct knowledge of Arktinos or Lesches, understood the *equus ligneus* to have been built starting from its sides and that these sides were made of fir. This description then appears to be confirmed a few verses later by a different description of the structure of the *equus ligneus*. In his depiction of the the inner structure of the contrivance, Vergil in fact notes that the *equus* was formed from *trabibus acernis staret* ('beams of maple')[81] and *roboribus textis* ('of oak').[82]

From an archaeological point of view, these short passages seem to refer directly to the building sequence of a *hull-based shell-first* ship. According to the archaeological evidence we have from ancient wrecks,[83] this reflects a shipbuilding tradition observed across the Mediterranean basin until at least the end of the Roman Empire.[84] Even the wooden species referred to in our textual sources – conifer for the planking, oak and maple for the internal beams of the skeleton – find a direct correspondence with the species that were in use in Mediterranean shipbuilding of that time.[85] With regards to the use of maple, while findings are limited, we do have evidence of its use in a shipbuilding context from the Punic Ship of the third century BC that was found in Marsala, Sicily,[86] where it is used for the sternpost.[87]

As for how the ἵππος was used, in Vergil's description, much as that set down by Homer, it is telling that the Trojans are said to have brought the *equus ligneus* into the citadel of Troy in terminology that specifically recalls the hauling of ships[88]

> Accingunt omnes operi pedibusque rotarum
> Subiciunt lapsus, et stuppea vincula collo
> Intendunt[...]

---

[79] Catullus, *Carmina* LXIV.9.
[80] Conington 1876; Austin 1964.
[81] Vergil, *Aeneid* II.112-113.
[82] Vergil, *Aeneid* II.186.
[83] Pomey, Kahanov, Rieth 2012.
[84] Pomey, Rieth 2005: 156-172.
[85] Rival 1991, Guibal, Pomey 2003.
[86] Frost at alii 1973, Frost 1981.
[87] Rival 1991: 73.
[88] Vergil, *Aeneid* II.235-237.

Everybody helps to put rollers under the machine
And to tie ropes around its neck.

The *rotarum* ('rollers') used to move the *equus* into the city appears to describe directly a well-known technique that was employed for moving heavy objects, particularly in battles, as is well known thanks to the descriptions of Tacitus (*subiectis rotis propellere*), for example.[89] The use of rollers rather than of fixing an item onto four wheels appears more evident still because of the choice of the verb *subicere*, which means 'to put under' and not 'to fix'. Furthermore, the use of a rope tied around the 'neck' would also support a reading of the *equus* as a ship; naval iconography of the Early Iron Age,[90] for example, shows ships with a rope around the neck of the animals, at the base of the figurehead. Even the description of the opening of the city wall recalls the use of hauling the ships at the end of the sailing season.[91] Vergil states in fact[92]

Dividimus muros, et moenia pandimus urbis

We separate the walls and remove the defence of the city

Usually translated as 'to break', the verb *dividere* can also be rendered as 'to separate'. Thus, we can argue that the author here is simply describing the action of opening a door, possibly by removing the architrave. Because of this action, potentially linked to the need to place rollers that would form a slipway along which the *equus* could be dragged, it would not be possible to close the fortress directly. This understanding finds further support in the description of the taking of the city of Troy: Vergil notes that, during the night, the Argives disembark from the hold (*cavo robore*) of the ἵπποϛ and open the doors of the city to their colleagues. Notably, however, they are not said to enter Tory through a breach in the city walls, but through the doors (portisque patentibus omins/accipiunt socios).[93]

Much as with the earliest narrative concerning the sack of Tory by Homer, it thus seems possible that many elements of Vergil's narrative suggest a close link between the creation and use of the ἵπποϛ and a maritime sphere. While it is therefore possible to render the Greek word ἵπποϛ not only as an animal, a horse, however, but also as a particular class of ship, this is not possible with the Latin translation, *equus*, that is employed by Vergil.[94] Nonetheless, the Latin playwright Plautus, writing in the third-second centuries BC certainly appears to have used the term *equus ligneus* to indicate a ship in one of his comedies (*nempe equo ligneo per vias ceruleas estis vecte*)[95], although this is only preserved in a much later source,[96] and it seems that there is much to argue that the term δουρατέοϛ ἵπποϛ led Latin writers to recall a class of ship. As we will see in later chapters, this is also a point that finds affirmation in other source material.

[89] Tacitus, *Historiae*. IV.23.
[90] Basch 1987: 309-10; Fontan 2014: 136.
[91] Blackman 2014.
[92] Vergil, *Aeneid* II.234.
[93] Vergil, *Aeneid* II.266-7. Johannes Lydus, in *De Mensibus* (490-557 AD) wrote '[...] others say that it [ἵπποϛ] was a gate with this name in Troy through which the Greeks entered' (Lydos, *De Mensibus*, 140 translated by Andrew Eastbourne for Roger Pearse in 2013).
[94] This could have been one of the reasons for the affirmation of the horse in Roman iconography of this event, a point that will be discussed in more detail in the next chapter.
[95] Plautus, *Rudens* I.5
[96] The text in question is reported in the *Lexicon Philologicum Praecipue Etymologicum et Sacrum in quo Latinae et a Latinibus Autoris*, which dates from 1655.

The Wooden Horse of Troy in Classical Art

The art of ancient Greece and Rome has provided us with many pictorial narratives of ancient myth and epic, as well as more strictly historical episodes. Such works thus offer contemporary insights into, and so a more precise idea of 'real' classical culture, as well as of the impact that these narratives must have had on their audiences across the centuries. Among the stories we can identify depicted on potteries or sculpted from bronze and marble, a particularly important role is held by Homer and the Homeric poems. Indeed, as Anthony Snodgrass, has noted, when we look at:

> the considerable list of unique or horrific actors which occur in the Trojan and other legends — scenes of battle between men and women, male duels with women looking on, the drudging of a body, the blinding of a giant, a men killing a woman or threatening to do so, the murder of a male-child, the sacrifice of a young woman — or extraordinary objects like the wooden horse[1]

it is apparent that the creation of these poetic works provided the ancient classical artists with an extensive repertoire on which to draws, at least from the Greek Archaic period. Within this remit, too, some subjects were examined, exploited, and represented with a particular frequency.

Despite Snodgrass's reference to the Trojan Horse as part of his wider commentary in the passage cited above, a wider analysis of the ancient iconography of the Trojan Horse[2] in fact suggests that this episode played only a minor role in the whole framework of ancient classical art, and particularly that produced in ancient Greece. This relative paucity of material might potentially be due to the lack of information provided by Homer concerning this particular episode: while the Trojan Horse is referenced a handful of times in the *Odyssey*, albeit with virtually no explanatory detail, the contrivance that was used by the Achaeans as a way of breaking the siege of Troy is in fact omitted almost entirely in the *Iliad*.

According to Brian Sparkes,[3] the lack of a proper description of the Trojan Horse in Homer's *Odyssey* might provide a key explanation as to why the earliest Greek vase-painters and artists rarely chose to reproduce this episode in their works. Equally, however, this same lack of anatomical and technological detail in Homer underpins the difficulty faced by modern scholars when trying to identify the precise inspiration behind those oldest images of the horse that are known to us,[4] and leads researchers to search for other primary source material that might have encouraged some of the first artistic depictions of the Trojan Horse from Greece. Certainly, until the point at which Vergil composed the *Aeneid*, it seems likely that interest in this scene must have been linked to some kind of minor narration or performance,

[1] Snodgrass 1998: 140.
[2] Sadurska 1986.
[3] Sparkes 1971: 56-57.
[4] In his discussion of the possible inspiration underlying the earliest known representation of the Trojan horse from Greek Art, the Boeotian fibula, Sparkes states: 'We should try to find an epic which might have inspired such an early representation of the Wooden Horse. Homer's Odyssey provides little encouragement'. (Sparkes 1971: 56).

and it thus seems sensible to search for evidence of such a scene, even if it is now lost or only partially known thanks to later texts.

When seeking to identify potential source material for the earliest depictions of the Trojan Horse, we first need to bear in mind some important elements that pertain more generally to the art of ancient Greece, as well as to the artistic introduction and use of mythic and epic themes. At least up to the end of the Geometric Period, painters and sculptors from Greece and the surrounding area did not seek to reproduce particular or recognisable scenes or events in their artistic creations. The appearance of the very first human and animal figures among the broader decorative themes reproduced on ceramics from Attica and Euboea in fact date to the Middle Geometric II period;[5] at this time, we can begin to identify the appearance of isolated animals, stylized in accordance with geometric tastes and patterns, as well as images of human mourners, which appeared on some Dypilon vases of the mid-eighth century BC.[6]

From the last part of the eighth century BC onwards, figured scenes became increasingly common, and it is possible to identify the first glimmers of an interest in reproducing narratives pictorially, an idea that was to become a central part of Classical Art. Towards the end of the Geometric period, heroes, and certain episodes with potential links to epic narratives finally started to become established as key themes within Greek art. However, as John Boardman has so clearly pointed out, 'on this threshold of full narrative art, it is easy to be over-optimistic and over-anxious to identify myth in what may be scenes of every day, of cult or of foreign inspiration'.[7] From the late seventh century BC onwards, the reproduction of heroic legends, and less commonly, divine mythology, on vases, began to increase, expanding throughout the archaic and classical period to reach a climax in the sixth century BC.[8] Nonetheless, it remains extremely difficult to identify with any certainty many of the figures to be reproduced on the ceramics from this period. Indeed, to interpret correctly many of these early depictions, it is also necessary to consider how the tales that are illustrated here then became significantly important to influence later vase-painters.

It is has often assumed by modern archaeologists and commentators that ancient artists, particularly vase-painters or sculptors, must have been literate, and therefore used to reading and interpreting ancient poems on a daily basis. In line with this thinking, scholars have often sought to identify precise matches between the extant written accounts of a story, and ancient visual representations of the same narrative. The problems linked to oral tradition, and the long-term circulation of narratives before they were first written down, and thus often at worst, ignored, or at best, underestimated. But, it has now become increasingly accepted, for the Homeric tales in particular, that the poems of Homer, as well as of many other poets of the archaic period, were composed and transmitted orally, and that audiences would have learned these myths and epics by listening to, or participating in oral performances and more

[5] Lippolis, Rocco 2011: 40-7.

[6] Boardmann 1994: 24.

[7] Boardman 1994: 27. Foreign inspiration undoubtedly plays a key role in the artistic evolution of themes and styles, as testified when examining the shift from Geometric style to Oriental influences on art in the seventh century BC. The growth in maritime contacts with the East and the colonies of the Western Mediterranean area, the development of a commercial relationship with the Phoenicians, and the introduction to some Greek centres of artisans and themes from the Levant all to an extent underlie the introduction of some particular objects like the sphinxes or lions into Greek culture (Markoe 1996).

[8] Snodgrass 1998: 140.

informal recitals.[9] Equally, however, we cannot exclude the possibility that 'vase painters may have learned their myths [...] at their mothers' knee',[10] and that the works they reproduced, many years later, were a visual version of what they remembered, rather than of what they had recently read. As such, and although it would seem more likely that novel versions of traditional tales typically tended to originate with poets rather than vase-painters,[11] we cannot deny that iconography and the visual narration of facts and myths might have introduced certain changes to the original story.

With regards to the Trojan Horse, the absence of a single original source, together with the changes that might have been introduced in reproductions, whether through artistic licence or memory, have contributed to the existence of a number of different visual variations of the tale that can be divided into at least three thematic groups: these broadly comprise the horse within the city walls or during the fighting that led to Troy's fall, the building of the horse, and the horse outside the walls of Troy or its entrance into the city.[12] These three groups together, however, include no more than thirty-seven figures from between the Late Geometric period and Late Antiquity,[13] and if we examine only those works dating from the oldest phases, it is in fact possible to note that there are only twenty-one different variations on representations of the Trojan Horse in Greek Art as a whole. This low number, particularly evident during the Late Geometric and Orientalising periods, appears to confirm that, despite its apparently crucial role in the events involving the Siege of Troy, the purported role played by the wooden horse received very little attention by artists from these early periods. It is possible that the editors found such a scene difficult to depict, not least due to the diverse — and often conflicting[14] — versions of the tale, narrated by at least four known poets during the seventh and sixth centuries BC[15] in the frame of the so-called Epic Cycle.

The iconography of the wooden horse in ancient Greece

The earliest known representation of the Trojan Horse is found on a poorly preserved Boeotian bronze fibula (Figure 10), now held at the British Museum in London;[16] the item dates from 700 BC, and possibly originated in Thebes.[17] Found together with the usual repertoire of images to be found on Boeotian fibulae of this period, such as birds, human figures, and fish, all of which continue to present elements typical of Geometric art from the eighth century BC,[18] there is a

[9] Hedreen 1996: 153-56, Boardman 1991: 82, Ervin 1964: 51.

[10] Boardman 1991: 82.

[11] Hedreen 1996: 153-54.

[12] These are the groups proposed by Sadurska in the iconographic study included in the *Lexycon Iconographicum Mythologiae Classicae* (Sadurska 1986). The order in which the groups are listed here reflects the chronology of the earliest depictions of each group.

[13] Sadurska (1986: 813-16) initially recorded thirty-six figures, but to this we can now add a new kotyle from Gela (Ingoglia 2000).

[14] We know that the size of the horse varied according to the imagination of the story teller: while Homer did not provide us with the exact number of the heroes hidden within the structure, Lesches of Mytilene, the author of the *Little Iliad*, placed it at three thousand warriors. Meanwhile Arktinos suggested a mere twelve warriors, Stesychorus, one hundred, and other authors fifty, thirty, or twenty-three or twenty-two (Ervin 1964: 54; Ingoglia 2000: 12-13, n. 38; Beschi 2013: 97).

[15] 'In the 7th – 6th centuries BC, at least four well known poets sung *Ilioupersis*: Arktinos and Lesches, Stesychorus and Ibykos and perhaps also Sakadas of Argos' (Ervin 1964: 51).

[16] BM 3205, Sadurska, 1986: fig. 22.

[17] Hampe 1936: 50-1, n. 101pl. 3.

[18] Basch 1987: 190-95.

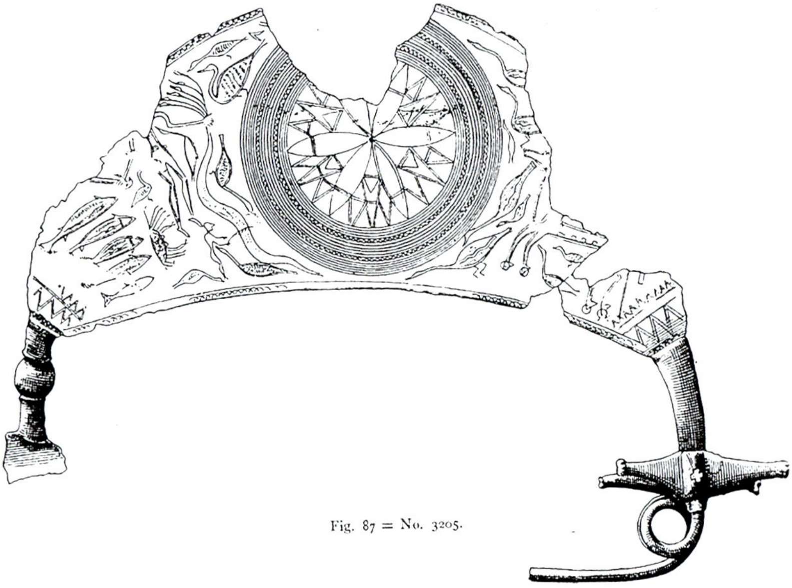

Figure 10. The Trojan Horse of the Boeotian bronze fibula – 700 BC.

Figure 11. The Trojan Horse engraved on the Pithos of Mykonos – 675 BC.

crescent-shaped bow, which appears to be a damaged image of the Trojan Horse, but on which nonetheless some interesting features are identifiable.

Based on a visual examination of the engraving, it is possible to point out the presence of four wheels, one apparently fixed at the extremity of each leg of the horse, as well as a series of at least four squared incisions in the lower part of the animal's belly, identified as the hatching. According to Sparkes' analysis, both the wheels and the hatching reveal 'instances of an artist seeking to make clear a story of which he knows the details'[19] — here, namely the need for the horse to be moved, and the presence of Achaean warriors inside the hollow, with the latter point confirmed by the presence of a group of armed men on the reverse of the fibula, potentially identifiable as the Greek troops who withdrew to Tenedos.[20] Although the image is badly damaged, a simple schematic on which the detail is difficult to read, this fibula nonetheless represents one of the earliest examples of a pictorial representation of a narrative in Greek art, and certainly we have no definite evidence of any legend or mythological representation before this period.[21]

The second clear representation of the horse, found engraved in relief on the neck of a pithos, a large ceramic storage container from Mykonos (Figure 11),[22] can be dated to 675 BC, while a small fragment, potentially from the leg of a similar horse, and thus usually interpreted as the Trojan Horse,[23] comes from another relief pithos found at Tenos, dated to 675-650 BC.[24] The Mykonos image is of particular interest because it appears on a pithos as part of a wider series of images of fights, duels, and battles, usually interpreted as scenes representing the sack of Troy.[25] As with the Boeotian fibula discussed above, the horse represented here shows wheels at the end of each legs, as well as square openings, each showing a warrior's head, visible on the side and neck of the horse. From four of these openings, the heroes also thrust out an arm holding an item of armour: respectively, a helmet, a shield, and two swords. Outside and around the horse are depicted soldiers who have apparently just jumped down from their hiding places; some are between the horse's legs, while others are superimposed over the horse's body, following two distinct orders.[26]

Both the vase from Mykonos and the small fragment of Tenos, are of Cycladic production and represent two samples of the local production of pithoi with figured decoration that belong to the so-called Tenian-Boeotian group,[27] which includes several samples from both Boeotia and the Cyclades. It is therefore possible that the shared iconographic link with the Boeotian fibula engraving could be more than coincidence; it may in fact indicate a similar source of inspiration for all these works. Certainly, the correspondence between the shape of the square openings along the horse's flank, together with the positioning of the wheels at the ends of the legs seems likely to derive from a common version of the tale. The fact that these very elements are lacking in the Homeric description of the horse, however, force us to search for an alternative source of the legend among other poems of the Epic Cycle known in the Late Geometric and Orientalising period throughout mainland Greece and the Island of Aegean.[28]

Analysis of the image of the horse, together with the other images reproduced on the body of the pithos, appear to suggest that all the scenes draw inspiration from the *Ilias Mikra*, one of

[19] Sparkes 1971: 55-56.
[20] Johansen 1967: 28-30.
[21] Sparkes 1971: 55; Snodgrass 1996: 140; Hedreen 1996: 154.
[22] Mykonos Museum 2240; Sadurska, 1986: fig. 23.
[23] The identification of this image as a possible Trojan Horse is largely due to the presence of a shield in the image, interpreted as 'one of the shields thrown by a Greek soldier from his hiding place' (Sadurska 1986: 315).
[24] Sadurska, 1986: fig. 24
[25] Johansen 1967: 56; Sparkes 1971: 56-57.
[26] According to Sparkes, the warriors shown on the upper level 'indicate that there were soldiers who took part in the sack besides the group that entered Troy in the Horse' (Sparkes 1971: 57).
[27] Ervin-Caskey 1976: 21.
[28] Ervin 1964: 51.

Figure 12. The Trojan Horse depicted on the Aryballos found at Caere – 560 BC.

the poems of the Epic Cycle,[29] attributed to Lesches of Mytilene.[30] Active during the seventh century BC, this poet, a native of Lesbos, was one of the post-Homeric poets producing works describing the last night of Troy. Unfortunately lost, known only through later fragments,[31] composition, usually dated to the third quarter of the seventh century BC[32] described the fall of Troy, and possibly provided some detail of the Trojan Horse.

According to some scholars,[33] the description of the wooden construction used to smuggle soldiers into Troy, with all its equine details, might also have been developed by Arktinos of Miletus in his *Sack of Ilion*,[34] another poet of the Epic Cycle whose work was in some way linked to that of the Lesches.[35] However, analysis of the different scenes[36] represented on the pithos still seem to suggest Lesches as the main inspiration for this vase.[37]

When we turn to the painted pottery, decorated with mythological scenes and produced in various centres in the period from the 7th to the 4th centuries BC, there are only a handful of representations of the Trojan Horse, and none of these representations apparently follow a precise iconography. Only in two cases, in fact, does the horse appear to be clearly depicted in the context of the last night of Troy; for the most part, in contrast, the painted potteries show the horse in a sacral context, usually involving the presence of certain deities, but with no direct link to the events recounted in epic verse, other than potential — and often inexplicit or minor — reminders.

[29] See infra *note 235* and *Chapter 3*.
[30] Ghali-Kahil 1955; Ervin 1964; West 2003: 15-16; Bielman Sanchez 2007.
[31] West 2003: 118-142.
[32] West 2003: 16.
[33] Beschi 2013.
[34] West 2003: 142-153.
[35] These two poets were involved in the legendary poetry competition, narrated in the legend of Phaenias of Eresus, who lived in the fourth century BC (Fantuzzi, Tsagalis 2015)
[36] Kahil (Gahli-Kahil 1955) has examined the so-called 'attack scenes', as inspired by the *Ilia Mikra*, in particular.
[37] Hedreen 1996: 170.

Dating from *c.* 560 BC,[38] around one century after the three depictions discussed above were created, a Corinthian aryballos (a perfume holder) was produced, found at Caere, in Etruria (Figure 12).[39] This image nonetheless appears to recall the image on the Mykonos pithos, at least in terms of the general context in which the image of the horse appears. On this small vessel, the horse is depicted encircled by naked warriors, who hold swords, javelins, and shields, positioned along three superimposed registers, and each showing the two counterparts.[40] Ten square hatches are shown along the body of the horse, close to the back legs, while a wooden ladder is used by some of the men as they exit the horse to reach the ground. Behind the horse, positioned alongside its tail ride three horsemen as they head towards the field of battle, while in front of it stands a statue of a big cat, which appears to be used by the Achaean troops as a convenient support as they climb out from the horse, along its head and neck,[41] and on to the cat itself as they climb towards the ground.[42]

Another figure of the wooden horse of Troy, found at Gela in Sicily, dates from 570/60 BC.[43] This image, depicted on a Corinthian kotyle, shows a horse with nine human heads protruding from its back, presumably in reference to the Achaean soldiers hidden within.[44] According to Ingoglia, the image represents the horse shown either outside the Trojan walls, as possibly indicated by the lack of wheels, or else located within the city just before the beginning of the battle, as might be suggested by the position of the last warrior, whose head is turned back, possibly to give 'a sign to the Achaeans waiting on the ships'.[45] As on the Mykonos pithos, however, painter has provided very few details of the location. Moreover, the number of warriors represented within the image does not correspond with the Homeric Epics. We must therefore question if some more minor version of the myth provided the inspiration for this image. Ingoglia[46] argues that this piece might reflect a direct knowledge on the part of the vase painter of Arktinos' version of the Troy Myth, composed during the sixth century BC. This suggestion finds some support in the correspondence between the number of heroes depicted on this vase and those listed by Vergil.[47]

Produced in the mid-sixth century BC, a small fragment of a black-figured vase, found at Orbetello in Etruria (Figure 13),[48] appears to represent at least four Greek warriors. The warriors in this image are leaving their equine hideout one by one by climbing on each other's shoulders. Once again, we cannot find a direct correspondence with the Homeric texts, nor with any other known version of the myth.[49] The anatomical accuracy of the horse's leg depicted on this fragment may, however, recall Arktinos' description of the horse, as we know

38 Sadurska 1986: 3815.
39 Sadurska, 1986: fig. 17.
40 Stanford, Luce 1974: 32, pl. 19; Sparkes 1971: f. 2.
41 According to Sadurska (1986: 815), some of the Achaeans in this representation are in fact leaving the horse through its mouth.
42 It should be noted that the cat was a principle element in Corinthian artwork of the Orientalising period, and thus its presence in this epic scene might simply reflect this general artistic context.
43 Fiorentini1994: 723.
44 Ingoglia 1999: 8-11.
45 Ingoglia 1999: 9.
46 Ingoglia 1999: 13.
47 Vergil, *Aeneid* II.261-262.
48 Sadurska, 1986: fig. 18.
49 Sadurska 1986: 815; Ingoglia 1999: 11.

Figure 13. The Trojan Horse of the black-figured vase found at Orbetello – around 550 BC.

Figure 14. The Carnelian scarab with the Trojan horse from Populonia.

Figure 15. The red-figured Attic cup of the Pittore della Fonderia – 480 BC.

that in the *Ilioupersis*, more precise features of this presumed war-machine were described, among them the structure of the legs and knees.[50]

Another small depiction of the horse appears on a find from Etruria, possibly from Populonia.[51] This is a carving on a carnelian scarab, now kept in New York (Figure 14),[52] in which the horse is represented upright on all four legs, while, around it, stand warriors wearing helms and bearing shields. A warrior's head, which protrudes from the base of the horse's neck, indicates the hatches, even though the author provided very few details of the horse aside from the anatomical elements.

Three Attic red-figure vases, all found in Etruria, can be dated to the fifth century BC. On one of these, a cup[53] attributed to the *Pittore della Fonderia* and dated 480 BC, we can see the horse being presented to the deities of Olympus by its creator, Epeius (Figure 15). The image of the horse does not, in fact, display any particular features that distinguish it as a weapon of war, but it can nonetheless be identified as the Trojan Horse thanks to the presence of Athena Pallas just behind it.[54] In similar fashion, Athena Pallas is also displayed with the horse in the other two Attic red-figure vases of the same centuries, the sole character to feature in these latter two works. But, while on the kylix of the *Pittore Saburoff*,[55] which dates from 470-460 BC and is now kept in Florence, the goddess is reproduced sitting before a great horse's head, which she adorns, on the amphora F 2415 from the same period, now preserved in Berlin, the deity is depicted completing work on a horse that is smaller than she, and is fixed to a squared base. As with the cup, these two figures do not offer any detail that could be connected to the myth of the Trojan war, and the horse itself could rather be interpreted as some kind of sacred attribute of Athena Pallas.[56]

According to Sparkes, these 'Attic vase-paintings have been thought to be versions of the Trojan Horse episode, though opinion on their relevance is divided'.[57] However, in the case of the amphora F 2415, in which the painter has included a square base beneath the horse's legs, it is arguably possible to draw a parallel between the figure reproduced on the pottery and one of the now-lost bronze statues produced during the Classical Period in Greece.[58] In his *Description of Greece*, Pausanias narrates that the first of these statues was on the Athens Acropolis, placed just next to the temple dedicated to Artemis Brauronia.

> ἵππος δὲ ὁ καλούμενος Δούριος ἀνάκειται χαλκοῦς [...]λέγεται δὲ ἔς τε ἐκεῖνον τὸν ἵππον ὡς τῶν Ἑλλήνων ἔνδον ἔχοι τοὺς ἀρίστους, καὶ δὴ καὶ τοῦ χαλκοῦ τὸ σχῆμά ἐστι κατὰ ταῦτα: καὶ Μενεσθεὺς καὶ Τεῦκρος ὑπερκύπτουσιν ἐξ αὐτοῦ, προσέτι δὲ καὶ οἱ παῖδες οἱ Θησέως.

---

50 Beschi 2013: 160-61.
51 Sadurska, 1986: fig. 30. It should be noted that the attribution of this gem, which comes from a private collection, remains in doubt (Sadurska 1986: 816).
52 Sparkes 1971: 58-59.
53 Sadurska, 1986: fig. 1.
54 Sadurska 1986: 813.
55 Sadurska, 1986: fig. 2.
56 According to studies of other Greek deities (see, for example, Nadal 2005 on Poseidon), the introduction of iconography of the horse as a sacred animal appears to have begun in the sixth century BC.
57 Sparkes 1971: 59-60.
58 Sadurska 1986: 816; Sparkes 1971: 60-61.

> There is the horse called Wooden set up in Bronze [...]. The legend says of that horse that it contained the most valiant of the Greeks, and the design of the bronze figure fits in well with this story. Menestheus and Teucer are peeping out of it, and so are the Sons of Thaeseus.[59]

This statue,[60] created by Strongylion, also appears to be reproduced on a small red-figure fragment[61] dating from the fifth century BC. Here, the front of a temple is represented, together with a possible statue of the horse with a ladder next to it.[62]

A second bronze statue,[63] also described by Pausanias, was found in Delphi. This was understood to have been donated to the temple by the Argives, possibly in 424 BC, as a sacred gift after a prediction by the Sibyl:

> τὸν δὲ ὑπὲρ τῆς καλουμένης Θυρέας Λακεδαιμονίων ἀγῶνα καὶ Ἀργείων, Σίβυλλα μὲν καὶ τοῦτον προεθέσπισεν ὡς συμβήσοιτο ἐξ ἴσου ταῖς πόλεσιν, Ἀργεῖοι δὲ ἀξιοῦντες ἐσχηκέναι πλέον ἐν τῷ ἔργῳ χαλκοῦν ἵππον—τὸν δούρειον δῆθεν—ἀπέστειλαν ἐς Δελφούς: τὸ δὲ ἔργον Ἀντιφάνους ἐστὶν Ἀργείου.
>
> The struggle for the district called Thyrea between the Lacedaemonians and the Argives was also foretold by the Sibyl, who said that the battle would be drawn. But the Argives claimed that they had the better of the engagement, and sent to Delphi a bronze horse, supposed to be the wooden horse of Troy. It was the work of Antiphanes of Argos.[64]

It is not possible to put forward a detailed interpretation of what such a statute might have looked like given the brevity of Pausanias' description. However, and based on what detail we do have, we might suppose that the sacred gift of the Argives was to some degree similar to the statue depicted on the red-figure amphora[65] in Berlin: that is, a simple horse, on a base, 'supposed to be the wooden horse of Troy', possibly because of the presence of an epigraph on the base.[66] The discovery of the sculpted base of the statue of the Trojan horse on the Athens Acropolis, — possibly that of the former statue described by the Greek geographer — might further support this interpretation.

Alongside these two statues, which might potentially be dated to the second quarter of the fifth century BC,[67] Pausanias also offers detail of another, now-lost image of the last night of Troy, believed to date from around the same time. While discussing the characters involved in the different versions of Sack of Troy, as narrated by different authors, Pausanias refers to the painting of the *Ilioupersis* by Polignotus,[68] which was on a wall of the Cnidian Lesche (the 'club-

[59] Pausanias, *Description of Greece* I.23.8.
[60] Sadurska, 1986: fig. 27.
[61] Sadurska, 1986: fig. 20.
[62] Sparkes 1971: 60-1.
[63] Sadurska, 1986: fig. 28.
[64] Pausanias, *Description of Greece* X.9.12.
[65] F 2415.
[66] It should be noted that in the preceding chapter of his *Description of Greece*, Pausanias refers to warships and naval battles, which might provide another possible link between the statue and the Trojan epic.
[67] Sparkes 1971: 59.
[68] Sadurska, 1986: fig. 21

Figure 16. Homeric bowl with the Trojan Horse – 3rd–2nd century BC.

house' of the Cnidians).[69] In this image, together with several heroes, the majority of whom were introduced to the Tory myth by Stesychorus or Kiprya, while others were invented by Polignotus himself,[70] the has also elected to include the builder of the Trojan Horse. Indeed, Pausanias writes, 'Epeius is [here] painted naked; he is razing to the ground the Trojan wall. Above the wall rises the head only of the Wooden Horse'.[71] The next such representations of the Trojan Horse in classical art did not appear for over a century; as more than one scholar has noticed,[72] there are in fact no known compositions to feature the Fall of Troy from the whole of the fourth century BC. The subject only seemed to find a resurgence, and a new and burgeoning popularity, in Hellenistic and Roman times, although by this time, the underlying narrative had also developed and expanded into different episodes.

According to Sparkes, in the third and second centuries BC, the scenes reproduced on the so-called 'Homeric Bowls' (Figure 16),[73] featuring horse and warriors positioned just outside the city walls Troy,[74] seem to have been affected by the iconographic influence of the illustrated manuscripts that began to be produced during this period.[75] The scene on the outer face of one such bowl, which is still complete, depicts various scenes from the Sack of Troy, among them a small horse, who no bigger than the humans that surround it, but that nonetheless features an opening on the side of its body. According to Sparkes, the variety of juxtaposed motifs would seem to indicate that we can possibly point to a now lost illustrated manuscript recounting one version of the sack of Troy for the artist's inspiration.[76] However, and as noted above, we equally cannot exclude the possibility that the individual who decorated this bowl elected to depict a series of scenes known from informal and oral circulation. According to

[69] Sparkes 1971: 59.
[70] 'Beyond these [heroes mentioned by Stesychorus and Ciprya] are painted on a couch Deinome, Metioche, Peisis and Cleodice. Deinome is the only one of these names to occur in what is called the *Little Iliad*; Polignotus, I think, invented the names of the others' (Pausanias, *Description of Greece* X.26.2).
[71] Pausanias, *Description of Greece* X.26.2. This is not the only painting of the Fall of Troy to be described by Pausanias: a second such work was in the Stoa Pokile in Athens (Pausanias, *Description of Greece* I.15.2). While it dated to the same period (Sparkes 1971: 59), this latter work did not portray the horse.
[72] Ingoglia 1999: 8; Sadurska 1986; Sparkes 1971: 61.
[73] Sadurska, 1986: fig. 25.
[74] Two Homeric bowls exist; one is complete, and the other is fragmentary (Sparkes 1971: 62).
[75] Walter 1962: 193-96.
[76] Sparkes 1971: 62.

West, in fact, we can assume that the artists who depicted these scenes 'were probably already using prose summaries' of the original poems of the Epic Cycle.[77]

Before moving on to explore the different Roman traditions that exist concerning the Trojan Horse, the majority of which seem to be strictly connected with the diffusion of Vergil's *Aeneid*, it is first necessary to summarize some general aspects of the Greek iconography that have been examined here. As we have seen, the very first images of the Trojan Horse appear at the beginning of seventh century BC, some four to five centuries after the events narrated by Homer, in a period that was characterised by the literary activity of some of the most important poets connected with the Epic Cycle. The effect of the Epic Cycle on the images of the Boeotian Bronze Fibula, as well as on the Pithos from Mykonos seems to be beyond doubt. The similarity between these two images, particularly their depictions of wheels at the bottom of each of the horse's four legs, together with the square openings inserted along the horse's body, seems to confirm that both artists must have been aware of at least one later narrative account of the last night of Troy, even though we cannot be sure that they knew a precise version of one of the poems of the Epic Cycle. According to Boardmann, in fact, 'vase painters might have learned their myths on informal occasions, at their mothers' knees or in street-corner banter, as well as from formal recitation of poetry'.[78]

Furthermore, as we have seen, the presence of other scenes, particularly of scenes of duels and violence, on the metopes that compose the narrative pattern of the pithos from Mykonos, not present in Homer's Iliad, make it possible to argue that one of the later poets and not Homer provided the inspiration for such early depictions. According to Hedreen, in fact, 'scenes like that of a warrior holding a sword, facing a woman and grasping the hem of her cloak while she stands, which have been called attack scenes, were grouped by Kahil with pursuit scenes as having been inspired by the Little Iliad of Lesches of Mytilene'.[79]

From an archaeological perspective, the cultural attribution of these very first images of the Trojan Horse is also of particular interest as we know that certain regions, among them Macedonia and Boeotia,[80] played a primary role in terms of introduction and dispersing horses across Greece, not only in terms of their artistic representation, but also at a very real, tangible level in terms of the use of the horse in war, games, and sacral contexts. It does not therefore seem entirely surprising that the idea of the Trojan Horse as an animal sacred to Athena might have developed in these lands, not least given that between the eighth and sixth centuries BC, this same area saw the development of the cavalry, for both a military and civic context.[81]

During the sixth century BC, the theme of the Trojan Horse, reproduced in accordance with earlier iconographic patterns of the previous century but equally increasingly influenced by the new sacral dimension awarded to horses,[82] appears to have spread outside Greece, a development that finds particular testament in the many different depictions produced at this time in Italy. Potentially, we might hypothesise that this particular subject, now firmly

[77] West 2003: 4.
[78] Boardmann 1992: 82.
[79] Hedreen 1996: 170.
[80] Schäfer 2005: 233.
[81] Drews 2010: 133; Anderson 1961: 13.
[82] Nadal 2005: 112.

established in Greek culture, began to be exported abroad as a way of celebrating the Greeks. Moreover, we cannot exclude the very real possibility that artists, working more than one century after the poets who produced the Epic Cycle, created and exported images of the narrative as they remembered it rather than as it had originally been recounted, thus reproducing the legend of the Trojan Horse in different ways across different images.

Moving into the fifth century BC, it would seem that imagery of the Trojan Horse began to reappear in Greece, but by this time — at least as regards vase painting — depictions of the horse had changed substantially. The Attic Red-figured-vases that we have seen thus show a small animal, usually displayed in a sacral context, positioned amongst several deities or else with Athena Pallas alone. In none of these scenes, however, is any direct reference made, either to known versions of the Sack of Troy, or to the Homeric texts themselves. On the other hand, however, it is possible to draw some interesting parallels with the images of sacred horses, as for instance with some of the figures of Pegasus and Poseidon,[83] as well as with the evolution of the iconography of ancient Greek horsemen.[84]

A study of classical iconography, then, would seem to suggest that in this period, the Wooden Horse of Troy had begun to obtain a symbolic value of its own, entering the Olympus. It is hardly coincidence that, as Pausanias testifies, this sacred contrivance was, during the fifth century BC, displayed in both a wall painting and as two bronze statues, all of which were placed in public and sacral contexts. As Bruno D'Agostino has argued the direct evidence of the dedication of horses to Artemis and Athena can be traced back to this century, and from this moment onward, these two goddesses, as well as certain other deities, often appear depicted together with these animals.[85] Moreover, by the 6th century BC, horses were perceived as sacred symbols of strength and power across Greece, in a way that was the case either at the time of the Trojan War itself, or of the first Homeric narrations.[86]

The iconography of the wooden horse in Rome

The existence of prose summaries like those that could have inspired the figured pattern of the Homeric Bowls discussed above might also be considered to underpin certain later images,[87] such as the horse sculpted on an alabastron funeral relief found in Etruria,[88] and now kept at the Archaeological Museum of Florence. In this presentation, the horse is located within the walls of Troy, and two armed warriors descend from a stair, while nearby, the Trojans are banqueting and drinking. On the *Tabula Iliaca Capitolina*, meanwhile, which dates to the first century BC,[89] the horse in fact appears twice. In the first image, it is depicted inside the city wall (Figure 17),[90] and a warrior holds a small ladder down which his comrades are able to exit the contrivance. Beneath the figure of the horse, an epigraph identifies it as the 'ΔΟΙΡΗΟΣ ΙΠΠΟΣ' (*horse made of wood*). Elsewhere, and in a different image, the horse is displayed together

[83] Drews 2010: 133; Nadal 2005: 115-132.
[84] Anderson 1961: 13.
[85] Nadal 2005, D'Agostino 2007.
[86] For example, as Drews (2010: 133) has noted, 'In the Homeric time, the myth of Bellerophon killing the Chimera did not include the intervention of the sacred winged horse Pegasus'.
[87] West 2003: 4 and note 2.
[88] Sadurska, 1986: fig. 29.
[89] Sparkes 1971: fig. 4.
[90] Sadurska, 1986: fig. 32.

Figure 17. The first representation of the Trojan Horse on the *Tabula Iliaca Capitolina* – 1st century BC.

Figure 18. The second representation of the Trojan Horse on the *Tabula Iliaca Capitolina* – 1st century BC.

with other characters known from the Trojan myth, among them Cassandra and Priamus, and both Greek and Trojan soldiers. The epigraph for this representation reads, 'ΔΟΥΡΗΟΣ ΙΠΠΟΣ' (Figure 18).

Far from being a mere question of linguistics, the shift from the original term ΔΟΥΡΑΤΕΟΣ (*made of planking*) of the Odyssey to ΔΟΥΡΗΟΣ (*made of wood*) is absolutely crucial for understanding both the source of inspiration for these latter figures and the proper nature of the horse itself. While for Homer, the ΙΠΠΟΣ (*hippos*) was ΔΟΥΡΑΤΕΟΣ (*made of planking*), in the sense of *made of wooden planks of the hulls (*ΔΟΥΡΑΤΑ*)*, in these depictions, we instead read ΔΟΙΡΗΟΣ or ΔΟΥΡΗΟΣ (*wooden*), in the sense of ΔΟΥΡΟ *(wood)*, that is, the far more general *made of the wood of the trees.* It would therefor seem that we cannot point to Homer for the inspiration behind these representations, but rather to later epic work, possibly even to one of the poems known by the Romans in the first century BC, such as that which inspired Vergil to make the myth of Aeneas the foundation to his legend of the birth of Imperial Rome. Interestingly, if we examine the find of a small fragment of a Megarian bowl from Volos,[91] which can be dated to between the 2nd century BC and the 2nd century AD,[92] it is notable that the use of this new

[91] Sadurska, 1986: fig. 26.
[92] Sadurska 1986: 816.

word had also entered into Greek culture. Inscribed on to this fragment, beneath the wheel fixed to the end of the horse's leg, it is possible to discern the letters ΔΟΙ.

By the first century AD, it would appear that the Legend of Troy had in fact definitively entered into Roman culture, where it has become one of the sacred and mythological stories used to decorate the walls of some private *villae* and *domus* of Pompei, as well as certain tombs and sarcophagi in Rome and elsewhere.[93] Notably, the choosing of this particular epic appears to be closely linked to the spreading knowledge of Vergil's *Aeneid*. Composed between 29 BC and 19 BC, and dedicated to the Roman Emperor, this poem effectively served as a foundation, fixing the cultural and sacral base of the imperial culture, by using the legend of Troy and identifying one of the Trojan heroes, Aeneas, as the ancestor of Roman people. It is no coincidence that the narrative of the events that permitted the heroes to reach the land of Rome began with what remains our most detailed narrative of the Fall of Troy.

Written some eleven to thirteen centuries after the events narrated by Homer, and no earlier than six to seven centuries after the presumed creation of the official written version of the Homeric epics, the *Aeneid* used multiple different sources, not all of which have been clearly identified, to describe the destruction of the citadel and the fashioning of the horse.[94] With regards to this latter point in particular, it is usually agreed[95] that Vergil's narration of this episode could have been inspired by direct knowledge of earlier texts pertaining to Homeric tradition, as well as to other Greek epics, primarily those of the Epic Cycle. R. G. Austin, in his detailed discussion of the text, has argued that different elements of the description given in the Latin epic make it possible to assume that Vergil must have been aware both of the *Ilioupersis* by Arktinos, and of the *Ilia Mikra* by Lesches.[96]

According to Proclus,[97] we can point to Lesches for the direct inspiration of the Vergil's description of the horse. Indeed, in his *Crestomatia*, in fact, Proclus summarizes the Lesches' description of the events as follows:[98]

> και ΄Επειός κατ Αθηνάς προαίρεσιν <άπό της'"ΐδης ζίιλα τεμών Αρ.> τον δονρειον ϊππον κατασκευάζει. Όδνσσενς τε άικισάμενος έαντόν <καί πενιχράν στολήν ένδνς Αρ.> κατάσκοπος εις "ΐλιον παραγίνεται- και αναγνωρισθείς υφ Ελένης περί της αλώσεως της πόλεως συντίθεται, κτείνας τέ τινας τών Τρωών έπι τας νανς άφικνεϊται. και μετα ταύτα συν Αιομήδει τό Παλλάδιον εκκομίζει εκ της Ιλίου.
>
> έπειτα εις τον δονρειον ϊππον τούς αρίστους έμβιβάσαντες, τάς τε σκηνάς καταφλέζαντες οί λοιποί τών Ελλήνων <καί καταλιπόντες Χίνωνα, ός έμελλεν αντοΐς πυρσον άναπτειν, της νυκτός Αρ.> εις Τένεδον ανάγονται, οί δε Τρώες τών κακών ΰπολαβόντες άπηλλάχθαι τόν τε δονρειον ϊππον εις τήν πάλιν είσδέχονται SieXoVreς μέρος τι τον τείχους, και ενωχοΰνται ώς νενικηκότες τούς "Ελληνας.[99]

93 Sadurska 1986: 814-816.
94 Barchiesi 1984.
95 Austin 1964: 1980; Rubino 2012.
96 Austin 1959: 16-25
97 Scafoglio 2004b: 39.
98 The translation of this text has been taken from M.L. West, 2003, 'Greek Epic Fragments from the 7th to the 5th centuries BC', Harvard University Press.
99 Proclus, *Chrestomathia*, suppleta *ex Apollodorus epitome* V.6-16.

> Epeios, following an initiative of Athena's, <fells timber from Ida> and constructs the wooden horse. Odysseus disfigures himself <and puts on pauper's clothes > and enters Ilion to reconnoitre. He is recognized by Helen, and comes to an agreement with her about the taking of the city. After killing some Trojans, he gets back to the ships. After this he brings the Palladion out of Ilios with Diomedes.
>
> Then they put the leading heroes into the wooden horse. The rest of the Greeks burn their huts and <leaving Sinon behind, who was to light a torch signal for them, in the night> they withdraw to Tenedos. The Trojans, believing themselves rid of their troubles, take the wooden horse into the city by breaching a portion of the wall, and start celebrating their supposed victory over the Greeks.

The direct link between Vergil and most of the images of the Roman era is clearly evident when examine images of the Trojan Horse produced in this period. Among the thirteen images of the Trojan Horse that can be dated to the Roman era, nine[100] depict the horse being pulled into the city, in accordance with the events narrated by Vergil:

> Accingunt omnes operi, pedibusque rotarum
> subiciunt lapsus, et stuppea vincula collo
> intendunt scandit fatalis machina muros
> feta armis. Pueri circum innuptaeque puellae
> sacra canunt, funemque manu contingere gaudent.
>
> One and all were girded for the task. Smooth-gliding wheels were beneath its feet; great ropes stretched round its neck, till over our walls the fatal engine climbed, pregnant with men-at-arms. On every side fair youths and maidens made a festal song, and hauled the ropes with merry heart and gay.[101]

Three frescos found in Pompeii portray this scene, two of which — one from the House of *Menandrus*[102] and the other one now on display at the Archaeological Museum in Naples[103]— show the horse fixed to a wooden platform and hauled into the city during a sort of ritual celebration (Figure 19). These images, which are clearly recalled in the famous paintings of Tiepolo now in London (Figure 20), as well as by scenes from the 2004 blockbuster *Troy*, starring Brad Pitt and Eric Bana, present several events, mainly linked to the need of an *Hollywoodian dramatization of the script*, that were not in the original Homeric version of the events (Figure 21). Furthermore, the artistic addition in the film of maidens throwing flowers, children singing, and musicians playing flutes seems to introduce a sacred element that draws together traditions from different cultures and times.

The presence of certain characters such as Priamus, Cassandra, and the Trojans,[104] into iconography, usually absent from the Greek portrayals described above, also seems to confirm the importance of Roman influence. Inspired by Vergil, the Roman depictions found at

[100] Sadurska, 1986: figg. 7,8,9,10,11,12,13,14,15.
[101] Vergil, *Aeneid* II. 235-239.
[102] Sadurska, 1986: fig. 9.
[103] Sadurska, 1986: fig. 8.
[104] Sadurska 1986: 814-16.

Figure 19. The Trojan Horse painted on the fresco of the House of Menandrus at Pompeii - 1st century AD.

Figure 20. The Trojan Horse on the painting by Tiepolo.

Pompeii, for example, do not celebrate the victory of the Achaeans, a people that the Roman 'can know as a whole, by knowing the crimes of a single one'.[105] Instead, they narrate the last night of the great ancestors of Rome: Priamus, Cassandra, Laocoon, and Aeneas himself, all considered here as victims of the 'Greek cheaters'.[106] The role of Cassandra in particular appears to have entered into Roman iconography together with the wooden horse: the Trojan prophetess is often depicted while attempting to prevent the entrance of the horse into the city.[107]

The most recent of the ancient depictions of the Trojan Horse to be examined here come from two manuscripts. On the *Codex Vergilius Romanus* (Figure 22),[108] an illustrated version of the *Aeneid* dated to between the fourth and the sixth centuries AD, the horse is represented next to a naked Sidon, who walks with some soldiers towards Priamus. In an image found in the Late Antique illuminated manuscript made in Rome in about 400 AD and named *Codex Vergilius Vaticanus*,[109] on the other hand, we can see the scene of the attack represented, with the Greek heroes exiting the horse during the night, just after the banquet, while the Achaean fleet stands still on the sea, waiting for the signal.

The analysis of the ancient iconography of the Trojan Horse presents certain peculiarities that are of particular great interest when trying to trace the development of a myth. First of all, in neither Greek nor Roman times does the figure of the horse follow a precise pattern, and it is very rare to find even two figures that appear to derive from the same source. Moreover, even in the very earliest images known to us, there does not appear to be a description that reflects the account given by Homer in the *Odyssey*; rather, even the oldest iconography reflects instead some of the poems from the Epic Cycle, namely those by Arktinos and Lesches. By the Roman era, artists were clearly looking instead to Vergil's *Aeneid* again a post-Homeric author, for the main inspiration, and his description of the events of the offal of Troy also drew directly on the Epic Cycle.

With the singular exception of the *Codex Vergilius Vaticanus*, the images of the Wooden Horse of Troy examined here make no reference to the Achaean fleet, nor to any of the Greek ships waiting, hidden, for the signal to attack the citadel. In other words, the maritime dimension of the Trojan War, as well as of the *Odyssey* itself, appears to have been lost from iconography as classical depictions of the Trojan Horse have developed. As Pausanias noted in his writings,[110] even in the classical period, the notion of the Trojan Horse was already become a legend in a very real sense, and it was not believed that real historical events necessarily matched artistic depictions. In this context, it is particularly interesting to note that in the first century AD, Pliny the Elder, while listing some of the most famous inventors in whole history in his *Naturalis Historiae*, attributed to the purported creator of the Trojan Horse, Epeius, the invention of the war machine known as a battering 'ram', thus implying quite a different use for his construction.[111]

[105] Vergil, *Aeneid* II.65-66.
[106] Vergil, *Aeneid* II.196.
[107] Sadurska, 1986: figg. 10,12,15.
[108] Sadurska, 1986: fig. 16.
[109] Sadurska, 1986: fig. 36.
[110] Pausanias, *Description of Greece* I.23.8.
[111] 'The battering-horse, for the destruction of walls, which is at the present day styled the "ram", was invented by Epeius, at Troy' (Pliny the Elder, *Naturalis Historiae* VII, 57).

Figure 21. The reproduction of the Trojan Horse created for the movie Troy, now at Cannakale.

For the Trojan Horse itself, the passage from history to legend appears to have been rapid: from the sixth century BC onwards, most of the images of the horse discussed here can be described rather as mythological or sacral depictions rather than historic representations. From an iconographic point of view, then, it is possible to draw a parallel with the development of epic narratives, which from the seventh century BC onwards saw the development of several new versions of the Sack of Troy, many of which involved different deities,[112] as well as in terms of descriptions of the Trojan Horse, which was transformed variously into a wooden statue, or presented as a sort of sacred simulacrum dedicated to Athena or to Poseidon.[113] This parallel between the evolution of iconography and of the narrative appears to have become more

[112] Beschi 2013.
[113] D'Agostino 2007.

Figure 22. The Trojan Horse on the *Codex Virgilius Romanus,* 5th century AD.

evident still during the Roman era, particularly from the second half of the first century BC onwards. Certainly, while the Fall of Troy, as presented in the second book of Vergil's *Aeneid*, effectively became the new and 'fixed' baseline for both the narrative and for successive iconography, Vergil's work also continued to influence later written accounts as well.

This certainly appears to be the case if we turn to Triphiodorus' *Sack of Troy*, written between the fourth and sixth centuries AD, for example. Here, for all that the author endeavours to describe the Horse by composing 'a poem so Greek that it could be imagined as coming from the mouth of Demodocus', depicting himself as 'the ultimate Homeric singer', and thus ensuring that he was 'not even remotely close to Vergil',[114] the poet nonetheless cannot envisage anything other than the legendary wooden horse of Vergil, for all that he plays on Pliny's idea that Epeius created a battering ram. While he aimed at a correct narration of the

[114] Miguelez-Cavero 2013: 70.

Trojan Myth, in accordance with earlier versions of the narrative, he therefore also tried to maintain a sort of internal coherence and verisimilitude and so enhance the credibility of his poem. Arguably, at the time that Triphiodorus was writing, the Roman Imperial audience for whom his work was intended had in fact achieved a balance between the serious reading of the physical world, as opposed to the ancient deeds narrated in the Homeric times, and the need to hear about local myths or pseudo-historical accounts. Already perfectly aware of Vergil's narration, Triphiodorus' readers therefore wanted to find, in this new Hellenocentric account of the events, some 'elements that could make the strategy of the horse credible, which is why the author described the construction of the horse with such care',[115] as well as introducing new ideas in his work.

If we turn back to Homer and his texts, however, it is evident that the lack of any direct correspondence between what was narrated by the author in the earliest works to describe the Fall of Troy, and the whole iconography of the horse that we have at our disposal, cannot be ignored. Yet arguably, this is not because Homer never mentioned this machine of war in detail; indeed, as various scholars have noted[116] there are several references to it in both the *Odyssey* and the *Iliad*. Crucially, however, as I shall go on to argue in the next chapters, in neither of those poems was the item described by Homer a horse, in contrast to those works by Arktinos and Lesches:[117] rather, the contrivance built by Epeius under the direction of Athena was a ship, a ship used to bear tributes after the war, in a practice that was quite common in the Bronze Age world.[118]

[115] Miguelez-Cavero 2013: 77.
[116] Snodgrass 1998; Franko 2006.
[117] Beschi 2013: 158-61.
[118] See infra chapter 1.

The *Hippos Ships* in the Ancient Mediterranean

Writing in about 400 BC, Xenophon, in the Economics, describes a Phoenician merchantman in the following way:

> καλλίστην δέ ποτε καὶ ἀκριβεστάτην ἔδοξα σκευῶν τάξιν ἰδεῖν, ὦ Σώκρατες, εἰσβὰς ἐπὶ θέαν εἰς τὸ μέγα πλοῖον τὸ Φοινικικόν. πλεῖστα γὰρ σκεύη ἐν σμικροτάτῳ ἀγγείῳ διακεχωρισμένα ἐθεασάμην. διὰ πολλῶν μὲν γὰρ δήπου, ἔφη, ξυλίνων σκευῶν καὶ πλεκτῶν ὁρμίζεται ναῦς καὶ ἀνάγεται, διὰ πολλῶν δὲ τῶν κρεμαστῶν καλουμένων πλεῖ, πολλοῖς δὲ μηχανήμασιν ἀνθώπλισται πρὸς τὰ πολέμια πλοῖα, πολλὰ δὲ ὅπλα τοῖς ἀνδράσι συμπεριάγει, πάντα δὲ σκεύη ὅσοισπερ ἐν οἰκίᾳ χρῶνται ἄνθρωποι τῇ συσσιτίᾳ ἑκάστῃ κομίζει: γέμει δὲ παρὰ πάντα φορτίων ὅσα ναύκληρος κέρδους ἕνεκα ἄγεται. καὶ ὅσα λέγω, ἔφη, ἐγώ, πάντα οὐκ ἐν πολλῷ τινι μείζονι χώρᾳ ἔκειτο ἢ ἐν δεκακλίνῳ στέγῃ συμμέτρῳ. καὶ οὕτω κείμενα ἕκαστα κατενόησα ὡς οὔτε ἄλληλα ἐμποδίζει οὔτε μαστευτοῦ δεῖται οὔτε ἀσυσκεύαστά ἐστιν οὔτε δυσλύτως ἔχει, ὥστε διατριβὴν παρέχειν, ὅταν τῳ ταχὺ δέῃ χρῆσθαι. τὸν δὲ τοῦ κυβερνήτου διάκονον, ὃς πρῳρεὺς τῆς νεὼς καλεῖται, οὕτως ηὗρον ἐπιστάμενον ἑκάστων τὴν χώραν ὡς καὶ ἀπὼν ἂν εἴποι ὅπου ἕκαστα κεῖται καὶ ὁπόσα ἐστὶν οὐδὲν ἧττον ἢ ὁ γράμματα ἐπιστάμενος εἴποι ἂν Σωκράτους καὶ ὁπόσα γράμματα καὶ ὅπου ἕκαστον τέτακται. εἶδον δέ, ἔφη ὁ Ἰσχόμαχος, καὶ ἐξετάζοντα τοῦτον αὐτὸν ἐν τῇ σχολῇ πάντα ὁπόσοις ἄρα δεῖ ἐν τῷ πλοίῳ χρῆσθαι. θαυμάσας δέ, ἔφη, τὴν ἐπίσκεψιν αὐτοῦ ἠρόμην τί πράττοι. ὁ δ᾽ εἶπεν: ἐπισκοπῶ, ἔφη, ὦ ξένε, εἴ τι συμβαίνοι γίγνεσθαι, πῶς κεῖται, ἔφη, τὰ ἐν τῇ νηί, ἢ εἴ τι ἀποστατεῖ ἢ εἰ δυστραπέλως τι σύγκειται. οὐ γάρ, ἔφη, ἐγχωρεῖ, ὅταν χειμάζῃ ὁ θεὸς ἐν τῇ θαλάττῃ, οὔτε μαστεύειν ὅτου ἂν δέῃ οὔτε δυστραπέλως ἔχον διδόναι. ἀπειλεῖ γὰρ ὁ θεὸς καὶ κολάζει τοὺς βλᾶκας. ἐὰν δὲ μόνον μὴ ἀπολέσῃ τοὺς μὴ ἁμαρτάνοντας, πάνυ ἀγαπητόν: ἐὰν δὲ καὶ πάνυ καλῶς ὑπηρετοῦντας σῴζῃ, πολλὴ χάρις, ἔφη, τοῖς θεοῖς.
>
> The most beautiful and accurate piece of arrangement, Socrates, that I ever remember seeing, was when I went on board the great Phoenician merchantman to look over her. For there I saw the largest number of things arranged in the smallest possible space. Now, it requires a great many things — oars and cordage — to put a ship into harbour and to take her out again; and a great deal of tackle too, as they call it, before she can sail along. She is equipped with many instruments of war against hostile vessels, and carries about many weapons for the men, having in her also for each mess all such appliances as are used in a house; whilst beside all this she has a heavy cargo, which the shipmaster takes with him to make profit on. In addition, all things that I am telling you of, said he, were stowed in a place not much bigger than a room in which ten dinner-couches could be comfortably set. Moreover, I observed that they were all so arranged that they did not get confused together, nor was there any need to hunt for them, since they were quite ready to hand and easily got at, to cause no delay when any one had sudden need of them. And then I found that the steersman's mate, the man at the prow, as they call him, knew where everything was so well, that even when not on the spot he could tell where each thing was, and how many of everything the ship had, as easily as a man who knows his alphabet can tell you the number of letters in "Socrates," and what their different places in the word are. And I saw, Ischomachus

> went on, this same man inspecting at his leisure everything ever used in the ship; and in some wonder at it, I asked him what he was doing; I, sir, said he, am inspecting the state of everything on board in case of an accident, to see if there is anything missing or not handy. For when Heaven raises a storm on the sea, said he, there is no time to look about for what you want, or to hunt for what is not at hand. For the Deity threatens the foolish-hearted, and punishes them; and if He refrain from destroying those that do no wrong, we must fain be content; while if He keep those that serve Him aright, we must render Heaven great thanks.[1]

These words, although written some centuries later than the Homeric narration of the Trojan Epic, clearly reflect the fact that in the Classical era, the Phoenicians were still considered to be great merchantmen and good sailors. While according to Oliver Dickinson 'the desire for metals [...] has often been specifically identified as the mainspring of Phoenician activity in the Aegean and the rest of the Mediterranean'[2], it is in fact possible to take this further, and to argue that, at least by the sixth century BC, the commerce of the Phoenicians embraced the furthest reaches of the known world.

As suggested by Xenophon, underlying the Phoenicians' role in the Mediterranean region was their renowned ability as sailors and shipwrights, an affinity with the sea that had its roots at least in the Bronze Age. Some of the earliest evidence found in the archaeological record of Phoenician merchant-ships includes the depiction of a ship on the wall of an Egyptian tomb,[3] now almost lost and only partially readable, and the image of four merchantmen painted in the Tomb of Kenamun at Thebe[4]. These paintings, all of which date from the end of the fifteenth century BC, and all of which were preserved within the tombs of Egyptian merchants and dignitaries, have usually been understood as to show ships of Syrian-Phoenician, rather than Egyptian origin,[5] and have been interpreted as providing direct proof for the presence of Phoenician-Syrian ships trading on the Nile.[6] The reason for identifying these ships as Syrian-Phoenician rather than Egyptian is two-fold: firstly, it reflects the lack of rope truss, which was typical, for example, of the sailing ships of the Queen Hatchepsut, and also corresponds to the particular structure of their sails, which have either straight or upward curving yards. Secondly, one of the most interesting and distinguishing elements of the hulls of these boats, as they are depicted in the paintings, are the end-posts at the two extremities of the ships. Almost vertical to the water-line, they give the hull a sort of symmetric structure that recalls the sailing vessels of the Eastern Mediterranean area during the Late Bronze Age, and in particular those of the Syro-Canaanite littoral,[7] rather than those of the Minoan or Mycenaean culture.[8] Thus, although these images were painted by unknown Egyptian artists and may

[1] Xenophon, *Economics* VIII.12-16. This translation is on Harvard 1938: 60.
[2] Dickinson 2006: 201. Further, according to Sherrat, the 'Characterisation of the Phoenician in the Iliad [...] as the carriers and traders of crafts and goods [...] suggests that, at one end of the archaeological spectrum, the name Phoenicians was probably first applied on the basis of the maritime activities of easterners in Aegean waters, rather than any real knowledge of or interest in where they might have come from. In this sense it could as well have applied to any Eastern Mediterranean Mariners' (Sherrat 2010b: 124).
[3] Muller 1904.
[4] Harvard 1938: 59.
[5] Casson 1971: 35-37.
[6] Faulkner, Davies 1947; Wachsmann 1998: 42-47.
[7] Wachsmann 1998: 39-60.
[8] Wachsmann 1998: 83-197.

recall directly the ships of the Pharaohs,[9] a closer analysis of their structure in fact enables us to confirm that the ships captured in these images must have been of Syrian-Phoenician origin, and were merely given an 'Egyptian look' by the artists who drew them.[10]

Used for sailing and conducting commerce around the Mediterranean coasts, the merchantmen used by the Phoenicians quickly ran to a good size, as some of the documents relating to the sea-commerce of the LBA of Levant testify. The Ugaritic letter 20.212, for example, clearly attests that in around 1200 BC, 2000 units of grain were ferried across the Gulf of Alexandretta in a single shipment.[11] Based on such evidence, we can reasonably conclude, as Casson has noted, that to load a Phoenician ship with some 450 tons of goods 'was by no means unusual'.[12] The discovery, in the 1980s, of a cargo wreck on the Turkish coast dating from the end of the fourteenth century BC has confirmed this interpretation, and has provided clear, physical evidence of how those ships were constructed.[13] It is no coincidence that the paintings from the tomb in Thebes have recently been studied and proposed as a basis from which to produce an ideal reconstruction of the hull of this wreck.

The link between Phoenicians and sea trading appears to have remained strong even some sixteen centuries after the Egyptian paints, discussed above, a point testified by Pliny the Elder. Writing during the first century AD, the Roman admiral noted the following while listing the inventors of different ship-types:[14]

> onerariam Hippus Tirius invenit
>
> Hippus the Tyrian invented the merchantman.

In this one short sentence, the author in fact appears to summarize two crucial elements of ancient naval history. Firstly, as we have just seen, by suggesting that the inventor of the merchantman was born in Tyre, Pliny confirms that this particular class of ship was still considered as being of Levantine origin during the Early Roman Imperial Era, probably due to the millennium-long tradition of commerce built up by the peoples of the Syro-Canaanite region. Secondly, by using the name *Hippus*, a name for which there is no correspondence at any point in Levantine history, Pliny seems to recall the *hippos ships* of Phoenician origin, a term of which he was probably aware due to a number of different sources, but in particular from the writings of the Greek geographer Strabo.

First studied in naval archaeology during the late nineteenth century,[15] the merchantmen of the Phoenicians are today well-known to scholars thanks to their appearance in textual and iconographic material, as well as through the analysis of material finds and study of ancient wrecks from across the Mediterranean world, and most notably from southern Anatolia and Spain. As we are now going to see, the possibility to refer to texts, images and wrecks has unveiled many of their features.

---

[9] Vinson 1994: 37-45.
[10] Casson 1971: 36.
[11] Nougayrol 1960: 165.
[12] Casson 1971: 36.
[13] Bass 1986, Pulack 1988, Bass et al. 1989.
[14] Pliny the Elder, *Naturalis Historia* VII. 57.
[15] Torr 1896: 113-14.

Textual evidence of the ἵππος ship

Even though we know many of the terms that were used by the Phoenicians to describe their ships and for the most part, to detail the ship's structural elements and fittings,[16] we still do not know what specific terminology was employed for those vessels that the Greeks defined as *hippos*. According to Strabo[17] the term *hippos* indicated a very specific class of boat that was characterized by the presence of a horse's head figurehead on the top of the stem-post. However, as will be explored below, it is in fact possible to expand on the information that we have about this particular ship-type from Strabo, and explore the role of the *hippos* in a broader setting.

From a chronological point of view, the earliest textual evidence that we can find referring to the *hippos ship* comes from Homer. In the *Odyssey*, as mentioned above,[18] Penelope is seen to state:[19]

> κῆρυξ, τίπτε δέ μοι πάϊς οἴχεται; οὐδέ τί μιν χρεὼ
> νηῶν ὠκυπόρων ἐπιβαινέμεν, αἵ θ' ἁλὸς ἵπποι
> ἀνδράσι γίγνονται, περόωσι δὲ πουλὺν ἐφ' ὑγρήν.
>
> Herald, why did my son leave? He did not need
> to sail on board of those fast ships, those that are the *hippoi*
> *of the sea* for the men, to run so much sea.

This dialogue between Penelope and the herald clearly seems to indicate that in these few verses, Homer refers directly to the *hippoi ships*. Examined against a broader reading of Homer's texts, we know that Telemachus, Penelope's son, had in fact embarked on a Taphian ship, that is, a non-Greek merchantman. Furthermore, as we are told some verses before, this ship formed part of a convoy of merchantmen that was travelling toward Temése, carrying iron and with the intention of trading copper (μετὰ χαλκόν, ἄγω δ' αἴθωνα σίδηρον).[20] This information would seem to indicate that the boat in question was involved in the mainspring of Phoenician activity in the Aegean and the wider Mediterranean during the Late Bronze Age and Early Iron Age.[21]

Some centuries after Homer, in the fifth century BC, the Greek playwright Sophocles recorded some further information about the *hippos ships* of the Archaic Mediterranean. In an extant fragment of an otherwise lost Tragedy, the *Andromeda*, Sophocles notes:[22]

[16] Stieglitz 1999: 412.
[17] Strabo, *Geography* II.3,4.
[18] See above, Chapter Two.
[19] Homer, *Odyssey* IV.707-709.
[20] Homer, *Odyssey* I.184.
[21] Sherrat 2010b: 124; Dickinson 2006: 201.
[22] Sophocles, *Andromeda*, frag. 2 Apud Athenaeum XI.64. There is a scholarly controversy about the interpretation of this fragment, going back to the ancient authors Atheaneus and Eustathius who took the word to refer to real horses (Pearson 1917: 81). However, as well stated by Cecil Torr, in this passage '*Sophocles was likely to select Phoenician types of ships, as the scene of the play was laid in Phoenicia; and both the* ἵπποι *and the* κύμβαι *are the very ships that Pliny associate with Phoenicians*' (Torr 1895: 114).

ἵπποισιν ἢ κύμβαισι ναυστολεῖς χθόνα

Do you travel toward the sea on-board hippoi or on small boats?

As has been pointed out by Torr,[23] this fragment is part of a scene set in a Phoenician context, and that features Phoenician characters and ships. Therefore, the decision to translate the word ἵπποισιν as *hippoi ships* rather than as *horses* would seem to make sense. In addition, the clear contrast made between the *big hippos* and the *small* boats seems rather to confirm that this ship-type was linked to open sea sailing and trading, thus creating a parallel with the ships of Levantine origin identified in the Egyptian paintings and Ugaritic texts.

In the second century AD, Strabo, in his *Geography*, whilst describing those men who had circumnavigated the African continent, also refers to a text by Posidonius, in which the author in turn writes of the travels of Eudoxus of Cyzicus:

> μνησθεὶς δὲ τῶν περιπλεῦσαι λεγομένων τὴν Λιβύην [...]ἀμάρτυρα δὲ ταῦτ' εἶναι φήσας καὶ Εὔδοξόν τινα Κυζικηνὸν θεωρὸν καὶ σπονδοφόρον τοῦ τῶν Κορείων ἀγῶνος ἐλθεῖν εἰς Αἴγυπτον ἱστορεῖ κατὰ τὸν δεύτερον Εὐεργέτην: συσταθῆναι δὲ καὶ τῷ βασιλεῖ καὶ τοῖς περὶ αὐτόν ... καὶ μάλιστα κατὰ τοὺς ἀνάπλους τοῦ Νείλου [...]τελευτήσαντος δ' ἐκείνου τὸν βίον, Κλεοπάτραν τὴν γυναῖκα διαδέξασθαι τὴν ἀρχήν: πάλιν οὖν καὶ ὑπὸ ταύτης πεμφθῆναι τὸν Εὔδοξον μετὰ μείζονος παρασκευῆς. ἐπανιόντα δ' ἀνέμοις παρενεχθῆναι ὑπὲρ τὴν Αἰθιοπίαν: προσφερόμενον δέ τισι τόποις ἐξοικειοῦσθαι τοὺς ἀνθρώπους μεταδόσει σιτίων τε καὶ οἴνου καὶ παλαθίδων, ὧν ἐκείνοις οὐ μετῆν, ἀντὶ δὲ τούτων ὑδρείας τε τυγχάνειν καὶ καθοδηγίας, ἀπογράφεσθαί τε τῶν ῥημάτων ἔνια. εὑρόντα δ' ἀκρόπρῳρον ξύλινον ἐκ ναυαγίου ἵππον ἔχον ἐγγεγλυμμένον, πυθόμενον ὡς ἀπὸ τῆς ἑσπέρας πλεόντων τινῶν εἴη τὸ ναυάγιον τοῦτο, κομίζειν αὐτὸ ἀναστρέψαντα πρὸς τὸν οἰκεῖον πλοῦν. σωθέντα δ' εἰς Αἴγυπτον, οὐκέτι τῆς Κλεοπάτρας ἡγουμένης ἀλλὰ τοῦ παιδός, ἀφαιρεθῆναι πάλιν πάντα:[...] τὸ δ' ἀκρόπρῳρον προφέροντα εἰς τὸ ἐμπόριον δεικνύναι τοῖς ναυκλήροις, γνῶναι δὲ Γαδειριτῶν ὄν: τούτων γὰρ τοὺς μὲν ἐμπόρους μεγάλα στέλλειν πλοῖα, τοὺς δὲ πένητας μικρά, ἃ καλεῖν ἵππους ἀπὸ τῶν ἐν ταῖς πρῴραις ἐπισήμων: τούτοις δὲ πλεῖν μέχρι τοῦ Λίξου ποταμοῦ περὶ τὴν Μαυρουσίαν ἁλιευομένους. ἀλλὰ τῶν δὴ ναυκλήρων τινὰς γνωρίσαι τὸ ἀκρόπρῳρον ἑνὸς τῶν ἀπὸ τοῦ Λίξου ποταμοῦ πορρώτερον πλευσάντων καὶ μὴ σωθέντων ὑπάρξαν.
>
> Posidonius, in speaking of those who have sailed round Africa [...] narrates how a certain Eudoxus of Cyzicus, sent with sacrifices and oblations to the Corean games, travelled into Egypt in the reign of Euergetes II. Being a learned man and much interested in the peculiarities of different countries, he made interests with the king and his ministers on the subject, but especially for exploring the Nile [...] On the death of Euergetes, his widow, Cleopatra, assumed the reins of government, and Eudoxus was again despatched with a richer cargo than before. On his journey back, he was carried by the winds above Ethiopia, and being thrown on certain [unknown] regions, he reconciled the inhabitants by presents of grain, wine, and cakes of pressed figs, articles, which they were without; receiving in exchange a supply of water, and guides for the journey. He also wrote down several words of their language, and having found

[23] Torr 1896: 114.

> the end of a prow, with a horse carved on it, which he was told formed part of the wreck of a vessel coming from the west, he took it with him, and proceeded on his homeward course. He arrived safely in Egypt where no longer Cleopatra, but her son ruled [...] He carried the prow into the market place, and exhibited it to the pilots who recognised it as being come from Gades. The merchant [of that place] employing large vessels, but the lesser traders small ships, which they style horses, from the figures of that animal borne on the prow, and in which they go out fishing around Maurusia, as far as the Lixus. Some of the pilot professed to recognise the prow as that of a vessel which had sailed beyond the river Lixus, but had not returned.[24]

As we can easily see from this text by Strabo, written in the second half of the second century BC,[25] Eudoxus' discovery of the first known wreck of a *hippos ship* provides us with some interesting information about the *hippos* ship-type from both a technological and a chronological point of view.

In terms of the name given to the ship, for the first time here we are told that the name *hippos* was linked to the presence of a horse's head figurehead on the ship's prow, carved on top of the stem post that decorated the forward end of the ship: ἀκρόπρῳρον ξύλινον ἐκ ναυαγίου ἵππον ἔχον ἐγγεγλυμμένον. With regards to the wreck's provenance, Strabo intimates that this particular ship-type came from the Western Mediterranean region, and was in particular associated with Gades, a Phoenician colony that was established at some point around the eighth century BC.[26] The boat-type in question was presumably used as a small merchantman, on which crews could travel the coast of North Africa towards north-western Morocco and down the River Lixus or, in at least one case, could actively circumnavigate the entire continent.

Even though there is no explicit record of any expedition around Africa that took place on-board a *hippoi*, we cannot ignore the fact that the most important account recording travel around the continent was that narrated by Herodotus,[27] which was in turn recounted by Necho II to the Phoenicians in around 600 BC. On this particular occasion, in fact, it would seem that the Pharaoh had issued the sailors with strict commands to return to Egypt via the passage of the Pillars of Hercules.[28] Although it is impossible to prove that the ships used for this voyage were Phoenician in style, we cannot ignore that — as many scholars have noted[29] — Necho is said to have built his war fleet in accordance with the Phoenician technology of the Triremes at that time.[30]

As far as we understand the ways in which these ships were used, it would seem based Strabo's information that by the second century BC, the primary function of these vessels

[24] Strabo, *Geography* II.3,4.

[25] The travel of Eudoxus can be dated to some point between the reign of Euergetes II (182-133 BC) and the end of the reign of Cleopatra (133-116 BC).

[26] Ribichini 2000.

[27] Herodotus, *Histories* IV.42.

[28] According to Hamilton and Falconer (1903, notes to the geography of Strabo), at the beginning of this narration Strabo directly recalls this expedition, even though '[the author] seems to confound the account (Herodotus IV, 44) of the expedition sent by Darius round southern Persia and Arabia with the circumnavigation of Libya (Herodotus IV, 42) by Necho II.

[29] Basch 1969: 230-9; Casson 1970: 340; 1971: 81; *contra* Lloyd 1975.

[30] Casson 1971: 81.

was for fishing. As has been pointed out by Medas,[31] this change in the use of the vessels, from trading to fishing, could well be linked to the progressive disappearance of the original hippoi ships, followed by a gradual hybridization of the local boats in which it might nonetheless be possible to identify some preserved traces of the original Phoenician ships. Nonetheless, we also cannot ignore a short fragment of writing by Euphorion of Calcydes from the late third century BC, but found preserved in the 6th century AD *De Mensibus* by Johannes Lydus, which seems to demonstrate that at the time that Euphorion was writing, the Greeks were still familiar with a merchant ship they named ἵππος.[32]

Some centuries later, as noted above in Chapter Two, the Latin playwright Plautus makes use of the Latin translation *equus* as a term with which to identify ships. It is no coincidence, then, that in Pliny's list of the inventors of ships and naval elements we cannot find any direct reference to the *equus*, apart from the already noted reference to the *hippos*.

> longa nave iasonem primum navigasse philostephanus auctor est, hegesias parhalum, ctesias samiramin, archemachus aegaeonem, biremem damastes erythraeos fecisse, triremem thucydides aminoclen corinthium, quadriremem aristoteles carthaginienses, quinqueremem *m*nesi*gi*ton salaminios, sex ordinum xenagoras syracusios, ab ea ad decemremem *m*nesigiton alexandrum magnum, ad duodecim ordines philostephanus ptolemaeum soterem, ad quindecim demetrium antigoni, ad xxx ptolemaeum philadelphum, ad xl ptolemaeum philopatorem, qui tryphon cognominatus est. onerariam hippus tyrius invenit, lembum cyrenenses, cumbam phoenices, celetem rhodii, cercyrum cyprii. siderum observationem in navigando phoenices, remum copae, latitudinem eius plata*eae*, vela icarus, malum et antennam daedalus, hippegum samii aut pericles atheniensis, tectas longas thasii; antea ex prora tantum et puppi pugnabatur. rostra addidit pisaeus tyrreni, ancoram eupalamus, eandem bidentem anacharsis, harpagones et manus pericles atheniensis, adminicula gubernandi tiphys. classe princeps depugnavit minos

> We learn from Philostephanus, that Jason was the first person who sailed in a long vessel; Hegesias says it was Paralus, Ctesias, Semiramis, and Archemachus, Ægeon. According to Damastes, the Erythræi were the first to construct vessels with two banks of oars; according to Thucydides, Aminocles, the Corinthian, first constructed them with three banks of oars; according to Aristotle, the Carthaginians, those with four banks; according to Mnesigiton, the people of Salamis, those with five banks; and, according to Xenagoras, the Syracusans, those with six; those above six, as far as ten, Mnesigiton says were first constructed by Alexander the Great. From Philostephanus, we learn that Ptolemy Soter made them as high as twelve banks; Demetrius, the son of Antigonus, with fifteen; Ptolemy Philadelphus, with thirty; and Ptolemy Philopater, who was surnamed Tryphon, with forty. Hippus, the Tyrian, was the first who invented merchant-ships; the Cyrenians, the pinnace; the Phœnicians, the passage—Boat; the Rhodians, the skiff; and the Cyprians, the cutter.

[31] Medas 2000: 87.

[32] Lydos includes this fragment together with a description of the '*hippos* gate' of the City of Troy, while listing the possible interpretation of the δουρατέος ἵππος. The author stated that for the ancient Greeks the ἵππος was a transport-ship (πλόιον).

> We are indebted to the Phœnicians for the first observation of the stars in navigation; the Copæ invented the oar, and the Platæans gave it its broad blade. Icarus was the person who invented sails, and Dædalus the mast and yards; the Samians, or else Pericles, the Athenian, transports for horses, and the Thracians, long covered vessels, — Before which time they used to fight only from the prow or the stern. Pisæus, the Tyrrhenian, added the beak to ships; Eupalamus, the anchor; Anacharsis, that with two flukes; Pericles, the Athenian, grappling-irons, and hooks like hands; and Tiphys, the helm and rudder. Minos was the first who waged war by means of ships.[33]

On the other hand, as has been pointed out by a number of scholars, we know that from at least the fifth century BC, a close relationship existed in Classical literature between ships and horses, as demonstrated by the notion of identifying the winged horse Pegasus with the representation of an oared vessel.[34] We cannot therefore assume that all descriptions of ships that make use of an equine terminology should necessarily be identified as *hippoi ships.* As we have seen, they need to be of Levantine origin, in use as merchantmen and, as Eudoxus suggested, styled with a horse-head carved on top of their posts to qualify for this description.

Iconography of the ἵππος ship

In the Phoenician world,[35] the lack of textual evidence pertaining to this particular class of ship is compensated for by the presence of several iconographic witnesses of hulls decorated by a horse figurehead and clearly recognizable as merchantmen of Levantine origin. These images come from the Assyrian area, as well as from the western area of Phoenician influence, particularly from southern Spain.

The very first representations of ἵππος ships can be found on the bronze bands that form the embossed decoration of the wood on the so-called Balawat Gate (Figure 23). Multiple finds of these bands were made between the late 19th century and the 1950s,[36] at the small site of Imgur-Enlil, the modern Balawat, and they belonged to the bronze decoration of a cedar monumental door, some of which were produced for Ashsurbanipal II (883-859 BC), but the majority of which were produced for the King Salmanasser III (858-824 BC).[37]

First published in the late twentieth century,[38] the oldest image to feature ἵππος ships appears to depict two vessels leaving and reaching a city, possibly the city of Tyre,[39] and setting sail for the coast during the reign of Ashsurbanipal II, in a sort of narrative continuum left-to-right. Onboard the ships, which clearly feature horse figureheads, people are featuring wearing pointed caps and turbans, as well as different clothes and mantles, but there is no indication of

[33] Pliny the Elder, *Naturalis Historiae* VII.56.
[34] Torr 1896: 114.
[35] The word Phoenician should here be understood as indicating the Eastern Mediterranean region (Bondì 1988, Bernardini 2014: 28-44) originating from the so-called Syro-Canaanite maritime culture (Wachsmann 1988: 39-60; Bernardini 2014: 9-16), as well as the Western Mediterranean region of Phoenician and Punic influence (Moscati 1988, Bernardini 2014: 57-70).
[36] Curtis, Tallis 2008.
[37] These bands are usually published and studied together. However, the Annals of the Assyrian kings inform us that they could have been part of different gates similar in shape (Grayson 1991: 189-91, 1996:5-6).
[38] Jacoby 1991: fig. 7.
[39] Jacoby 1991: 118-19.

Figure 23. The Balawat Gate. Reconstruction at the British Museum.

any element of the load. According to Jacoby and Barnett,[40] the ship on the left displays the horse-head decoration only on the stem-post, while the right hull features both the stem-post and sternpost. The inscription above the scene mentions the city of Tyre.[41] The ship on the right is depicted being hauled up onto the beach, as suggested by the presence of a rope tied around the end-post, at the base of the neck of the horse figurehead.

Even though the authors who first wrote about this image originally interpreted it as a showing a scene of tribute bearers from Tyre during the reign of Ashsurbanipal II,[42] the figure arguably seems to better recall the scene narrated by a stone in Ashsurbanipal's North West Palace in Calah, the main city of his reign.[43] The people shown disembarking from the ships, all dressed in different western costume,[44] arguably look more like some of the guests invited by the king to the banquet that was held when the palace of Calah was consecrated,[45] and it is possible that they are portrayed while bearing gifts rather than tribute. On that occasion, in fact, as Ashsurbanipal II wrote in the annals that he had invited '47,074 men [and] women [...] from every part of my land, 5,000 dignitaries [and] envoys of the people of the lands Suhu, Hindānu, Patinu, Hatti, Tyre, Sidon, Gurgumu, Malidu, Hubušku, Gilzānu, Kummu, [and] Musasiru, 16,000 people of Calah, [and] 1,500 zarīqū of my palace'.[46] Even though we cannot know the exact year of the building of the cedar gate of Imgur-Enlil, this figure can be attributed to the second quarter of the ninth century BC.

A more precise dating can, however, be suggested for two of the bands of decorations found on the cedar gate of the Imgur-Enlil palace, built and decorated for Salmanasser III from 850 BC

[40] Jacoby 1991: 119: fig. 7 and n. 16.
[41] It is to stress that this inscription, mentioned by Jacoby (1991), did not enter the list published by Grayson (1991).
[42] Jacoby 1991: 118-19.
[43] Grayson 1991: 288-93.
[44] Wäfler 1975: 77-117.
[45] Grayson 1991: 288.
[46] Text: A.0.101.30; l.140-150.

Figure 24. One of the Band of the Gate with the *hippos ships* – 859 BC.

Figure 25. The second Band of the Gate with the *hippos ships* – 859 BC.

onwards.[47] Referring to two different campaigns led by the king against the people of the 'sea-coasts', these images portray the tribute delivered by the defeated city of Tyre and are dated to the Phoenician Campaign of 859 BC.[48] According to the Great Inscription on the gate, at the end of this campaign, Salmanasser III received 'the tribute of the kings of the sea-coast'.[49]

The first band (Figure 24), which was initially published in 1878,[50] and which is now divided between the Louvre and the Walter Arts Museum at Baltimore, features two merchantmen loaded with precious items, which are then hauled from the sea to the walls of a city, probably that of Salmanasser III. Originally interpreted as riverine boats,[51] these two ships have more recently been identified as ἵππος *ships* thanks to a re-analysis of the broader context in which the image occurs.[52] In this relief, in fact, we can see people bearing tribute to Salmanasser III on board two boats, both of which are decorated with horse-head figurehead on-top of their abaft and ahead posts. As has been pointed out by Fontan, the individuals who bring the tribute are dressed in a costume that is 'Phoenician in style, composed of a pointed cap

[47] Grayson 1996: 27.
[48] King 1915: 23.
[49] Text: A.0.102.5, II, l. 3-5
[50] Lenormant 1878.
[51] Lenormant 1878: 128.
[52] Basch 1987: 305-06; Fontan 2014.

and with a long mantle slipped over a tunic'.[53] Furthermore, the text that is incised above the procession scene reads:[54] 'I received tribute from the cities of the People of Tyre and Sidon: Silver, Gold, Tin, Bronze, Wool, Lapis Lazuli and Carnelian'.[55] This appears to confirm the Phoenician identity of both tribute-bearers and ships.[56] The recent re-assemblage of the band to its complete state[57] has allowed this interpretation of the image to be confirmed.

The second band (Figure 25), which was discovered some years later and is now kept at the British Museum,[58] presents a similar scene, with a couple of ships depicted as leaving the city of Tyre[59] in order to bring the agreed tribute to the Assyrian king after his Phoenician campaign of 859 BE. In this sample, again, the identification of the boats as ἵππος *ships* is supported by the presence of the two horse-head-figureheads on the two end-posts of the hulls, by the *Phoenician* costume worn by the tribute-bearers, and by the inscription, which reads: 'I received Tribute from the Boats of the People of Tyre and Sidon'.[60]

In combination, the ships represented in these bands show some kind of narrative continuum: from right to the left in the former, and left to right in the latter, it is possible to follow the loading, shipping, hauling and unloading of the tribute. Moreover, all of the ships depicted in the two reliefs clearly have both end posts decorated, always with a horse-head figurehead carved on their top, and both pilots and crew are dressed in Phoenician costume. Inside the ships, the load is composed of metal ingots and exotic objects such as elephant tusks, in accordance with the information reported in the Bible[61] and this material appears to be regularly stowed onboard the vessels. Finally, as in the depiction of the ships sent to Ashsurbanipal II, the images here bear witness to the use of ropes tied around the stem-post, at the base of the neck of the horse-head figurehead, in order to run the hauling operation.

A third band from the gate of Salmanasser III shows a scene that might conceivably refer to one of the Babylonian campaigns of the king, particularly to the receipt of the tribute from Adinu of Bit-Dakkuri, dated 850 BC.[62] This relief shows two small ships, which are depicted while crossing what appears to be a stream, with some objects regularly stowed on-board and a in individual paddling at the prow. The two end-posts of the hulls are almost vertical to the water line, as in the images described above. Furthermore, while the sternposts appear to be free from any decoration, the upper ends of the stem-posts of both these vessels seem to preserve a shaped ornamentation, possibly a carved figurehead, even though their poor state of preservation makes it extremely difficult to interpret them accurately. However, as with the ships in the first three bands, in this case image the forward hull is once again depicted being hauled by means of a rope that is tied at the base of the prow figurehead.

[53] Fontan 2004: 137.

[54] I use here the translation first presented by Grayson (Grayson 1996) and recently reprised by Fontan (2014: 137). That the argument put forward by Béatrice André-Salvini (1991) that the words *Wool, Lapis-Lazuli* could be translated into *Purple Wool* should, however, be noted. In addition, in the first edition by Lenormant, the French scholars responsible for the edition suggested translating this phrase as *Wool and Precious Onyx* (Lenormant 1878)

[55] Grayson 1996: 147; Text: A.0.102.84

[56] Eelat 1977.

[57] Fontan 2014.

[58] King 1915: pl. XIII.

[59] Jacoby 1991: 118-22.

[60] Grayson 1996: 147; text: A.0.102.66.

[61] The Holy Bible, *Ezekiel* XXVII.12-24.

[62] King 1915: 23; Grayson 1996: 145.

Figure 26. The relief of the Palace of Sargon II at Khorsabad – 705 BC.

According to the Great Inscription of the Gate, the image relates to the payment of a tribute that resembles those made by the people of Tyre discussed above: the tribute appears to have comprised 'silver, gold, bronze, tin, iron, and elephant hides',[63] a point that also appears to be confirmed by some other inscriptions found in the palaces of Salmanasser III.[64] Furthermore, as with the Phoenician Campaign, this occasion, the Second Campaign of Babylonia, the texts of the king again inform us that, when the Assyrian monarch received the tribute from Adinu of Bit-Dakkuri, it was received 'from the king of the Sea-Land'.[65] Thus, even on this occasion where there is a lack of very clear evidence to point to the presence of the horse-head figurehead, it still cannot be excluded that the two ships engraved in this band are ἵππος ships.

Dating to around one century after the Balawat Gate is the most famous representation of ἵππος ships yet known in Assyrian art, found on a relief at Sargon II's Palace at Khorsabad (Figure 26). Built in the last quarter of the 8th century BC, the Palace was constructed between 707 and 706 BC.[66] It was adorned by reliefs devoted to the celebration of the successful campaigns of different kings,[67] and it featured images of timber transport on the forefront.[68] The city of Khorsabad was very much a reflection of how Sargon wished to be perceived,[69] and so the decision to display this particular scene at the entrance of the new palace is of particular interest, as it celebrates what the king considered to be one of his greatest successes: the control of the timber trade from the West. As has been pointed out by Linder, on this relief 'more than one achievement of the king is commemorated: his large-scale building activities [...]; the use of [...] boats for the lumber transport; the employment [...] of [...] specialists in the nautical professions'.[70]

[63] Text A.0.102.5, VI, l. 5-7.
[64] Grayson 1996: 31, 37, 46.
[65] Text A.0.102.5, VI, l. 8. This interpretation of the text appears in King 1915 (p. 20) and not in the edition of the texts by Grayson.
[66] Elayi 2017: 207-10.
[67] Tadmor 1958: 22-40; Reade 1976: 95-104.
[68] Albenda 1983, Linder 1986.
[69] Reade 1979: 342.
[70] Linder 1986: 280.

Figure 27. *Hippos ship* of the Khorsabad Relief.

Figure 28. *Hippos ship* of the Khorsabad Relief.

The importance of timber supply becomes particularly evident even through a reading of the Assyrian texts that refer to the city of Khorsabad. In these, the city is often described as home to 'palaces of ivory, maple, boxwood, mulberry, cedar, cypress, juniper, lime and pistachio-wood'.[71] As we can easily imagine, the Neo-Assyrian control of these western trading routes must have included the boats and vessels of the Phoenicians and the Cypriots. Even though the Phoenician cities were not much affected by Sargon's conquest of the West, not least as the vast majority had already fallen under an Assyrian sphere of influence some decades earlier after being subjugated by Tiglat-Pileser III around 738 BC,[72] they nonetheless played an important role in Sargon's strategy, with Simirra and Tyre of particular importance. Departing with his fleet from their coastal harbours, the king reached Cyprus and the open sea, where

[71] Text: ARAB 2.84. In another text, Sargon celebrates his capital city in which he founded "a park like into Mount Amanus, in which were set out every tree of the Hittite-Land, the plants of every mountain" (ARAB 2.83)
[72] Elayi 2017: 67.

he could trade with the kingdoms of the eastern Mediterranean and establish control on his western borders.[73] It is no coincidence that it was during the rule of Sargon that Neo-Assyrian texts for the first time all mention the rulers of the *hinterland*, those of the *seashore* and those of the *midst of the sea.*[74]

From a naval perspective, the relief shows fourteen merchant ships[75] that are depicted transporting lumber from the west, probably from the Mediterranean coasts of the Phoenicians[76] or from the mountains east of Lebanon[77] up to the city of Sargon. All of the ships depicted have a flat-bottomed hull, with ends curving upwards at both prow and stern (Figures 27 and 28). On all of these, the forward ends are decorated by means of a horse-head figurehead carved on top of the stem-post, while the sternpost is in the form of a flower. Even though Linder interpreted these boats as being uniquely for riverine use, designed specifically for this purpose by Phoenician shipwrights who worked for the Neo-Assyrian king and who employed the same principles in their construction as had been used for in 'wooden river boats which were sailing the Euphrates and Tigris for millennia',[78] there are nonetheless several elements that enable us include these ships among the Phoenician merchantmen that the Greeks called ἵππος.

With regards to their general shape, while these hulls differ from those of the Balawat bands because of the difference in the decoration of the two end-posts, they nonetheless find a close parallel for this in other Phoenician seagoing vessels. The analysis of the ships engraved on the relief at Nimrud Palace, constructed during the reign of Tiglat-Pileser III (r. 745-727 BC)[79], and of the oared vessels of the relief from the Kuyundijk palace of Sennecharib (r. 705-681 BC) highlight some interesting similarities. In particular in this latter figure,[80] which illustrate the ships that were used by the king of Tyre and Sidon Luli to leave his reign after his defeat, the hulls feature of the end-posts in the form of a flower and the other one decorated with an animal-head, but here it is not in the form of a horse, but of a bird.[81]

Seven of the ships of Khorsabad,[82] all depicted moving from right to left, show their load of trunks stowed both over the deck and partially laid along the stern, with four to five oarsmen as crew. Three vessels,[83] which sail from left to right, have the rigging tied to the two end-posts and the mast folded surmounted by a possible main-top, or a basket, both rectangular[84] and in the form of a flower.[85] At the two ends of the figure, in panels 1 and 3, we can recognize some vessels on which the load of trunks is being loaded or un-loaded. The image to the right

[73] Elayi 2017: 67-78.
[74] As Elayi has noted, during the rule of Sargon "the Phoenician cities were also regarded as *Hatti*, a general term that at that time designated the population of the near east" (Elayi 2017: 68)
[75] Botta 1849: pl. XXXIII; Basch 1987: 308-9, fig. 650 A-C.
[76] Albenda 1983.
[77] Linder 1986.
[78] Linder 1986: 281.
[79] Basch 1987: fig 652.
[80] Layard 1849, I.71; Barnett 1956: pl. XXII b.
[81] The presence of the bird head on top of the post allowed Basch (1987: 311-18) to draw a parallel with the ships of the Sea Peoples.
[82] Basch 1987: fig. 650, n. 2, 7, 9, 10, 11, 12, 14.
[83] Basch 1987: fig. 650, n. 1, 5, 8.
[84] Basch 1987: fig. 650, n. 1, 5.
[85] Basch 1987: fig. 650, n. 8.

Figure 29. Relief of Ashurbanirpal III at Kuyunijk. *Hippos ship*. 669-626 BC.

end of the scene[86] represents its crew preparing the hull for loading, and operating to remove the rigging after having unfolded the mast, while in the image on the left, crews are depicted as unloading the trunks from the last three ships on to land.[87]

According to different scholars[88] the transport of wood depicted on this relief follows a maritime route from the Phoenician forests or Cyprus across to Assyria, passing probably through Tyre,[89] Arwad,[90] and the mouth of the Orontes – possibly close to Al-Mina –and then along the Euphrates. The men on-board the vessels are dressed in typical western costume,[91] some of them with the traditional Phoenician pointed cap.

In addition to this relief on the forefront, two more ἵπποϛ ships appear at Khorsabad on the decoration of room 7.[92] Similar in shape to those of the former panels,[93] they show the two stem-posts decorated by means of a horse-head figurehead that is sculpted, together with the sternpost, without any additional decoration. The hulls are revealed to be empty, with no traces of mast, rigging, or oars. The identification of these vessels as Phoenician seems to be supported by the shape of the figureheads of the ships, as well as by the presence of a fortified city on an island rich in wood, which supports the suggestion of a Mediterranean location.[94]

Another ἵπποϛ ship is depicted on a relief at the Kuyundijk Palace of Ashurbanipal III (Figure 29),[95] as part of a reproduction of a lion-hunting scene. The scene is located on a possible

[86] Basch 1987: fig. 650 n. 13.
[87] Basch 1987: fig. 650 n. 3, 4, 6.
[88] Albenda 1983, Elayi 2017: 67-70 contra Linder 1986.
[89] Elayi 2017: 67.
[90] Elayi, Elayi 2005: 129-33.
[91] Wäfler 1975: 77-117.
[92] Layard 1849, II, pl. 114.
[93] Basch 1987: 309.
[94] Elayi 2017: 67-68.
[95] Salonen 1939: pl. XIX, 2; Barnett 1956: pl. XXII.a.

river[96] or else in the Babylonian marshes,[97] and it features an oared vessel with two oar-lines superimposed, the upper one with the oars placed just over the gunwale, and the lower one with a series of round holes or ports along the bulwark. At the stern, two rudders are featured, one on each side of the vessel managed by a pilot; while on the deck, a series of archers and armed warriors hunt lions by means of arrows and lances as shown in the prow section. A captured lion is tied up at the back of the boat. The hull presents the two end-posts as upturned and almost vertical to the water line. The forward post is decorated with a horse-head figurehead, thus making it possible to identify the boat as a proper ἵππος *ship*, while toward the stern of the boat, the end-post protrudes inwards towards the hull, and is decorated at its top by a carved animal-head, but notably not a horse.

Dated to between 669 BC and 626 BC, the rear end of this vessel appears different to those of the previous samples from Balawat and Khorsabad. However, the round stern section of the hull and the inward turning of the sternpost directly recall some the Phoenician ships depicted on the relief of Sennecharib, dated 705-681 BC, as well as from Kuyundijk,[98] and Nineveh.[99] Despite having a mixed propulsion method of both oars and sail, as seen in the Ashurbanipal scene, the ship depicted in this panel also presents two superimposed rows of oarsmen and a series of round holes along the bulwark to host the oars. Once again, the presence of two different animal-head figureheads finds a close parallel in another relief that features a presumed Phoenician vessel sailing in the Mediterranean. This occurs in a relief from the Nimrud Palace of Tiglat-Pileser III,[100] dated 745-727 BC, which shows 'a mast with a top-mast identical to those of the Khorsabad relief'.[101]

Also from the Levant, but occurring outside of the Assyrian world,[102] are two small images of ἵππος *ships* that appear on a seal discovered in Jerusalem, although unfortunately these results are not yet published.[103] An additional image appears on a seal that comes from a private collection.[104] These seals both date to the 8th century BC, and they provide important information about the use and diffusion of this class of vessels during the Iron Age.

The analysis of the iconography of the first image makes it possible to include these two figures among the images of merchant ships that can possibly be used to identify some elements included in the cargo for trading activities. According to the information provided by Professor Kahanov, the stamp from Jerusalem, which shows a hull with a prow figurehead carved with

[96] Basch 1987: 318.
[97] Barnett 1956: 228.
[98] Basch 1987: 313, n. 659; Barnett 1956: pl. XXII.b.
[99] Basch 1987, n. 654.
[100] Basch 1987, n. 652.
[101] Basch 1987: 309.
[102] A recent paper (Friedman 2015) has even proposed that a man-of-war, sculpted on a relief from Kentape that is attributed to the reign of Tiglat Pileser III (745-727 BC), should number among the ἵππος ships . This identification, based on the parallel with the gold rings of Moclhos (1500-1450 BC) and the so-called Ring of Minos (1450-1400 BC) is rejected here. On the one hand, the presumed horse-head *aphlastron* of the Assyrian boat does not in fact display a horse-head decoration. On the other hand, the two gold rings, both pertaining to the Minoan world, do not show war-ships and their aft ends are not decorated with carved animal heads, as assumed by the author: rather, they include the typical weathervane of the Minoan *aphlastron* (Wachsmann 1998; Basch 1987). Finally, as we know from textual and archaeological evidence, the ἵππος ships were Phoenician merchantmen and not men-of-war.
[103] I am extremely grateful to Professor Yakhov Kahanov of the Leon Recanati centre for Archaeology of the University of Haifa for having sent me the picture and description of the yet unpublished stamp found in Jerusalem, and to his successor, Dr Debrah Cvikel, for allowing me to mention the discovery in this text.
[104] Avigad 1982.

Figure 30. A *hippos ship* depicted on a Hebrew seal of the 8-7th centuries now in a private collection.

a horse-head, appeared in association with a group of objects of Phoenician origin, possibly identifiable as a prince-gift, a donation, or some kind of tribute.

At the same time, the seal studied by Avigad (Figure 30) is also of great interest. Of scaraboid form, and possibly obtained from a hard stone, the seal presents a Hebrew inscription that is surmounted by a depiction of a merchant ship; both inscription and drawing are encircled by a line that traces an oval shape, as is common for the Hebrew seals of the eighth century BC. The two-line inscription reads, 'Belonging to ʾOniyahu – Son of Merab', and is written in the semi-cursive formal Hebrew that is typical of inscription dating to the eight and seventh centuries BC.[105] An analysis of the text suggests that this seal refers to a merchant, whose name, ʾOniyahu, can be interpreted both as 'Yahweh is my ship' or as 'The Ship of Yahweh', a play on words that may well have justified the adoption of the merchantmen as the heraldic symbol[106] of his seal.[107]

With regards to the ship itself, the stern appears to be equipped with a steering oar. A series of round dots in a single row along the bulwark presumably reproduce either the ports, or protection for the oarsmen, as seen on the relief of Sennecharib at Kuyundijk.[108] However, no oars are shown in use, so that the vessel should presumably be interpreted as relying on sail power. A single mast amidship, supported fore and aft by the rigs, carries a square sail on a possible yard. At the stern, the end-post is almost vertical to the waterline, decorated by a possible vegetal motif; at the prow, the stem-post shows a carved figurehead in the form of a horse-head. According to Avigad, in an interpretation that has now been widely accepted, this seal reproduces 'an Israelite ship [...] which seem to have been merchantmen fit for long voyages [based on] Phoenician prototypes'.[109] Furthermore, as suggested by Casson, this figure is considered to be the sole proper representation currently known of a sailing ἵππος ship: carved on a Hebrew seal, of Israelite origin, this type 'has obviously been borrowed by some of the Phoenicians' neighbours'.[110]

[105] Avigad 1982: 59.
[106] The use of a symbolic/heraldic figure to illustrate a name is attested on two other Hebrew seals of the same period (Avigad 1966: pl.4c; Avigad 1981: 57.3).
[107] Avigad 1982: 60.
[108] Basch 1987: 313, n. 659; Barnett 1956: pl. XXII.b.
[109] Avigad 1982: 60-61.
[110] Casson 1994: 41.

Figure 31. The vase in form of *hippos ship* found in the site of El-Carrambolo.

In the Western Mediterranean Sea, two finds attest to the presence of this ship-type from at least from the 8th century BC. The first one is a boat-shaped vase discovered in the Phoenician sanctuary of El-Carrambolo (Figure 31), in Southern Spain, not far from the Phoenician colony of Gades. According to the stratigraphy of the site, the vase comes from the level of the so-called IV Sanctuary, where a number of objects were found that point to a sacred use of this area.[111] Included among these was a fragment of Greek pottery of Attic production, attributed to the Middle Geometric II phase and dated to the first half of the eighth century BC.[112] This date has been confirmed by a radiocarbon dating of some samples of vegetable elements from the same layer, which have provided a date of between 810 and 791 BC,[113] making this latter date a *terminus post quem* for this phase of use of the IV Sanctuary.

From a naval perspective, the presence of a moulded line along the centre of the vase indicating the keel confirms the identification of this object as a boat model. Furthermore, the presence of a horse-head figurehead at one end of the model would seem to suggest that the boat could be identified as a prototype of a ἵππος ship.[114] A second moulded horse-head found on the same site, in a contemporaneous layer and made of the same clay as the vase,[115] seems to suggest that both ends of this boat-shaped vase were originally decorated, thus drawing a parallel with the Assyrian reliefs of the Balawat Gates . Along one of the bulwarks on the model, four circular holes in the ceramic hull just under the gunwale appear to indicate the position of some of the oar-stations, even though no traces of the eventual removable-oars have been found.[116] On the opposite bulwark, the presence of a moulded ring, created just over the gunwale and not far from the figurehead, points to the ritual nature of the vase. Even the general round shape of this ship model should be seen largely as a product of the

[111] Guerrero, Escacena, 2010: 242.
[112] Escacena *and alii*, 2007: 7-16.
[113] Guerrero, Escacena, 2010: 246.
[114] Escacena *and alii* 2007: 11; Guerrero, Escacena, 2010: 243-46.
[115] Escacena *and alii 2007*: 11-12.
[116] Escacena *and alii* 2007: 9-11.

Figure 32. The gem of the Aliseda Treasure with a *hippos ship.*

functional deformation of the vase rather than a technological element of the prototype; this interpretation would seem to find confirmation in different boat-shaped ritual vases of the Western Mediterranean area of the Early Iron Age.[117] Nonetheless, and for all its simplicity, this figure provides us with solid evidence of the presence of this kind of boat in the Iberian peninsula during the Early Iron Age.

This conclusion also fits neatly with the findings suggested by the formal analysis of the second find from the west, at Aliseda (Figure 32). This latter find, a gem decorating a gold ring, was part of a wider hoard found in the sacred site of Aliseda.[118] The find was discovered in association with elements pertaining to a sacred context imported in Spain during the Early Iron Age, and discussion of the gem itself, and its identification as an ἵππος ship was first published by Barnett.[119] According to Aubet, the treasure hoard should be interpreted as a Princes' Gift,[120] and offers direct proof of the commercial activities of the seventh century BC along the east-west route. The dating of the assemblage has thus been widely discussed, although without the support of a proper archaeological context. Almagro Gobrea[121] dated this sacred context to the third quarter of the 6th century BC, while Nicolini,[122] following the interpretation by Aubet, has proposed a date from the first half of the seventh century. A recent re-analysis of the hoard has led to its interpretation as being of 'Phoenician, Greek or at least Oriental origin'.[123] A date has thus been proposed of 'between the end of the 7th – beginning of the 6th century BC' for the hoard's creation, even though in this princely gift, objects some decades older can also be identified, 'voluntary collected because of their value'.[124]

[117] Escacena *and alii* 2007: 9-13.
[118] Aubet 1994.
[119] Barnett 1958: pl. XXIV.b.
[120] Aubet 1994: 251.
[121] Almagro Gobrea 1977.
[122] Nicolini 1991.
[123] Celestino Salgado 2007: 590; Celestino, Blanco 2006: 119.
[124] Celestino, Salgado 2007: 597-98.

In terms of the gem itself, the hull of the ship is reproduced by means of a single line incision, and it shows the two ends upturned, both decorated by a horse-head figurehead. Amidships, there is a mainmast, although no sails are depicted. At the stern, a possible pilot handles a steering oar, while ahead of the mast, a second human figure sits on some kind of chair – possibly the depiction of a cabin. The general shape of the hull in the image, which has inevitably been strongly conditioned by the dimensions and shape of the gem itself, recalls several Levantine figures of ships from Babylonia and the Levant,[125] so that its cultural attribution to the Phoenician sphere of influence appears out of doubt. According to Barnett, this image should be considered as a direct proof of the presence of the ἵππος ship in the Western Mediterranean in later times, some decades after the Assyrian reliefs, when 'it seems to have died out in Phoenicia proper, but survived, chiefly for fishing, near Cadiz'.[126] As we have seen, some classical texts refer to the longevity of this particular ship-type in the Mediterranean. With regards to its representation in iconography, a carnelian gem from the third century BC, probably coming from Sidon[127] and now at the Museum of Haifa,[128] provides us with a new evidence of the use of the ἵππος ship along the Phoenician coast of Levant into the second half of the First Millennium BC. The ship has an elongated hull, with an animal-shaped figurehead, possibly a horse, on its stem-post. At the stern, the end-post is carved in a sort of fishtail shape.[129] Six oars protruding from the starboard bulwark indicate that these were used to power the boat: their position and alignment underneath the gunwale evoke that of the oars depicted on the relief of Sennecharib at Kuyundijk.[130] Two dolphins complete the maritime scene on the upper part of the gem; their tails recall the decoration of the ship's sternpost. Unfortunately, information about the archaeological context of this find is lacking, making it difficult to draw firm conclusions, even though its cultural attribution to Tyre,[131] one of the most important Phoenician cities of the First Millennium BC, seems to support the identification of this ship with a ἵππος ship.

From the 3rd Century BC on, the lack of any further image of this particular boat type from across the Mediterranean Basin confirms what we can also identify in the written sources: as suggested in the analysis of the text by Pliny the Elder, which states 'onerariam Hippus Tirius invenit',[132] while we cannot exclude the possibility that knowledge of this ship-type survived in memory, it appears that at least by the Classical era, the direct knowledge of its features was lost. Therefore, the idea of interpreting some later vessels as possible ἵππος ships, particularly those from Palestrina, Neumagen, and Arras[133] should be rejected. These images pertaining to different cultural worlds, particularly the Hellenistic and Roman, and they clearly show different boat-types in which they only thing they hold in common with the Phoenician ἵππος ship is the presence of an animal-shaped figurehead at the prow. However, the depictions of these boats suggest that they lack all the other ethnic, structural, and functional elements

[125] Salonen 1939: pl. III.
[126] Barnett 1958: 228.
[127] Friedman 2015: 25.
[128] Ringel 1984: fig. 51.
[129] According to Friedman, the prow should form a forward projection of the keel line, interpreted by the author as a 'constructional element to provide better hydrodynamics and stability or [...] a stylized ram' (Friedman 2015: 25). However, while on the one hand we have to exclude the presence of the ram on a merchantman, on the other hand, the shape of the connection between the keel and the stem-post of this ship directly recalls those of Khorsabad.
[130] Basch 1987: 313.
[131] Friedman 2015: 25.
[132] Pliny the Elder, *Naturalis Historiae* VII.56.
[133] Friedman 2015: 26-28.

that were so typical of the Phoenician vessels. A structural analysis of the boat of the Nile from Palestrina, a big cabin-carrier,[134] for example, makes it clear that this cannot be considered as one of those boats 'from Gades, [used by] the merchants [...], which had sailed beyond the river Lixus, but had not returned', to which Strabo referred.[135]

Direct evidence of the ἵππος ship

A confirmation of Strabo's narrative comes from the sea of Southern Spain: in the bay of Mazzaron, in a context of clear Phoenician influence,[136] the discovery of two small wrecks (*Mazarròn 1* and *Mazarròn 2*) — one of which was virtually complete — has shed light on the technical structure of the ἵππος ships used in the Western Mediterranean Sea during the Early Archaic period. Produced locally, these boats offer many interesting insights into Iberian shipbuilding technology of this time, as well as reflecting the impact of Phoenician technology on local production.[137] More pertinently still, their analysis has led to a reconsideration of the information obtained from other Mediterranean wrecks, including those from earlier periods, which have revealed interesting new information about the possible origins of the ἵππος ships, their usage, and the spread of this ship type across the region.

First discovered in 1988 and then excavated during different campaigns between 1998 and the early 1990s, the *Mazarròn 1* wreck was lying on the seabed in the small bay of Mazarròn. The area was characterized by the presence of several fragments of pottery, most of which were from amphorae of the *Trayamar 1* type. These finds have enabled the archaeological context to be dated to between the end of the seventh and the beginning of the sixth century BC.[138] At the time that the wreck was discovered, the keel of the hull, at about 4.5 m in length, was still preserved, together with the remains of nine planks and with four frames just over the planking. While still connected to this frame, the planking, carvel-built and assembled by means of a series of pegged mortise-and-tenon joints on which the mortises were carved at mid-height into the seams, had 'almost completely lost its original profile'.[139] According to the analysis made during the first excavations, some of the strakes still showed light traces of vegetal stitches, even though it was not possible to recognize the relics of a proper sewing system on a part of the planking. On the contrary, the contemporary presence of these two systems — both mortise-and-tenons and sewing — on the same planks has enabled scholars to interpret this overlapping of the assembling solutions as a way either to reinforce the water-tightness of the hull, or else as the consequence of a repair, rather than as a technological choice to make use of a mixed structure.[140] Some holes for stitches were identified for the connection between the third and the fourth strakes, and the end-post.[141]

The excavation also allowed analysis of the keel (shaped and with a quadrangular section, chamfered but not rabbeted), a possible stem-post (unfortunately now lost), and some

[134] Friedman 2015: 26.
[135] Strabo, *Geography* II.2,3.
[136] Negueruela 2005: 22-23.
[137] Pomey 1997: 91-93; Negueruela 2005: 27-31.
[138] Negueruela, Ortiz 2004: 228-29.
[139] Negueruela 2005: 24.
[140] Negueruela *and alii* 1995: 189-92.
[141] De Juan 2014: 27.

elements of the non-active framing. These frames, which were apparently 'round in section',[142] were connected to the hull by means of ligatures made of vegetal fibres, which passed through circular holes and were X-shaped. Some of these ligatures were still visible, while the absence of some of the frames has permitted scholars to verify the presence of the four passing holes that were used to connect the framing to the planking, as well as the presence of a coating system, made of a mixture of pitch and wax.[143]

The *Mazarròn 2* wreck, first revealed in 1999 and located not far from the wreck of *Mazarròn* 1 in the the bay, was discovered lying under a layer of *posidonia oceanica* whose radiocarbon dating (2760±30 BP and 2490±30 BP) has confirmed the chronological attribution based on the archaeological context.[144] As with the first wreck, the presence of many fragments of amphorae of the *Trayamar 1*[145] type found around the boat, together with a sample of this particular class of objects found inside the hull, have allowed the vessel to be dated to the end of the seventh or beginning of the sixth century BC.[146]

The wreck is 8.15 m in length, 2.20 m in width, and is very similar in shape to the *Mazarròn* 1. A hull-based vessel, the boat was built shell-first, with a central keel of *Cypressus Sempervivens L.* that was connected to the stem-post and the sternpost by means of simple scarfs. The bulwarks, both sewn to the end-posts, preserve nine strakes made by planks of *Pinus*, and assembled by means of a series of mortis-and-tenons joints that were fixed with pegs made from *Olea Europea* and were inserted from the inside of the hull. The frames, all of *Ficus Carica*, were fixed to the planking by means of X-shaped ligatures, obtained thanks to vegetal fibres that passed through four round holes in two planks.[147] A removable mast-step was located just over the keel and blocked on the framing by means of some shaped scarfs. A squared mortise next to a hole shaped for hosting the wedge that fixed the mast and four smaller holes for the stanchions seem to confirm that the mast could be folded and unfolded.[148] Inside the hull, and initially covered at the time the wreck was discovered by a part of the load, were four beams, two of which were used as thwarts. Towards the stern, one of the beams (beam number 2) had two holes at one of its ends, not far from the gunwale, used 'to install the rudder'.[149] Outside the hull was a wooden anchor, with a lead stock still in place and a broken fluke, not far from the bulwark, and 'connected to the hull with a vegetal rope'.[150]

From a technological point of view, the technology underpinning the design of these two wrecks pay witness to a local tradition that was nonetheless clearly influenced by elements coming from other cultures. As demonstrated through the technical analysis of the woods

[142] Negueruela *and alii* 1995: 195.
[143] Negueruela *and alii* 1995: 196.
[144] Negueruela *and alii* 2000: 1674.
[145] The amphora has been recently attributed to the type 10.2.1.1 of Ramon, and identified as produced in Malaga (Minano 2014: p. 10)
[146] Negueruela *and alii* 1995: 192; Negueruela 2005: 26-28. De Juan has proposed that this wreck should be dated to the last quarter of the seventh century BC due to the presence of the virtually complete amphora, 're-used on the hull' (De Juan 2014). However, this precise dating does not seem to be supported by other parameters.
[147] Negueruela, Ortiz 2004: 236-237.
[148] Negueruela 2005: 39 and fig. 21.
[149] Negueruela 2005: 26.
[150] Negueruela 2005: 26. The presence of the anchor, and of the pottery on-board the boat, seem to confirm that both this boat, and *Mazarròn* 1, might have sunk while they were stationed inside the bay, which was a place both known and used by local fishermen and traders (Negueruela *and alii* 1995: 192-93).

used, both ship hulls are derived from the same architectural family — the Iberic-Family[151] — suggested by the presence of residual stitches, while at the same time, the use of the mortise-and-tenon joinery indicates the use of hexogen solutions, particularly those of Phoenician origin.[152]

The discovery and study of the Mazarròn boats has also helped to shed light on a wreck found at Golo, near the isle of Corsica, during the nineteenth century.[153] The analysis of the dossier written by the excavator in the late nineteenth century,[154] and particularly of the unpublished files,[155] has made it possible to compare some of the drawn elements from Golo with those studied at Mazarròn. According to Pomey, the boat found in Corsica can be considered as a type of sister-ship to *Mazarròn* 2 and therefore of 'Iberic tradition with a strong Phoenician influence, [...] dated to the 7th-6th century BC, due to the architectural elements of its joinery as well as to the connection between planking and framing'.[156] Despite the loss of almost every wooden element, the existing files and drawings make it possible to interpret this wreck as a ship of about 15 m in length and with a decked prow section.[157] The presence of a rectangular unrabetted keel, 15 cm moulded and 18 cm sided, connected to the end-posts by means of two locked keyed-hook scarfs,[158] together with the use of a mortise-and-tenon joinery for the planking, both seem to point to the influence of Phoenician shipbuilding. At the same time, the framing, with transversal timbers spaced between 0.5–1 m apart and rounded in shape, the removable mast-step, almost identical to that of *Mazarròn* 2, as well as the use of vegetable stitches to fix the frames to the hull, all point to an Iberian tradition.[159] As it is bigger than *Mazarròn* 2, the Golo wreck is the best indication currently available as to the kinds of big merchantmen, strongly influenced by Phoenician traditions, that were used by the inhabitants of Southern Spain to trade around the Mediterranean and that were remembered by Strabo some centuries later. As an early relative of the Cala Culip wreck,[160] this hull is effectively the 'step-nephew' of the earliest merchantmen we know from the Mediterranean Sea and the 'step-sister' of the ἵππος ships

In the early seventies, some years after the discovery at Cape Gelydonia of one of the oldest mortise-and-tenon wrecks to be discovered across the whole Mediterranean,[161] George Bass described the cultural attribution of this wreck in the following terms:

> Copper ingots, more valuable than pottery but not so lasting, have been regarded as typical Minoan trade goods because of an Egyptian tomb painting of such ingots arriving from 'Keftu': a dozen such paintings, however, refer to the ingots as being Syrian, and in one case even brought to Egypt on a Syrian ship. [...] The route westward from Syria, known from a Ugaritic document, passed by Alasia (Cyprus?), Western

[151] De Juan 2014.
[152] Pomey 2009; 2012.
[153] Paris 1892.
[154] Nucci, Orsini 2003; Dell'Amico 2008.
[155] Pomey 2012.
[156] Pomey 2012: 27-28.
[157] The presence of a series of beams confirm the construction of the deck. However, we do not have enough extant elements to suggest what a reconstruction might look like.
[158] Pomey 2012: 22.
[159] Pomey 2012: 23.
[160] Polzer 2014.
[161] Bass 1964; 1969.

> Cilicia and Lycia to 'Kaphtor' (Crete). A Canaanite ship, with Cypriot cargo, was following this route when it sank in 100 feet of water near Cape Gelydonia in Lycia [...] A fifteenth-century BC ingot carrier, following the same route, sank while crossing the bay of Antalya, Between Cilicia and Lycia. Another, of the same date, lies in the sea near Cymae in Euboea.[162]

One decade later, the discovery of the Ulu Burun wreck,[163] with its marvellous loads, did not simply confirm this idea: rather, through the presence of a portion of the wooden hull, which was preserved thanks to the presence of a great amount of copper ingots apparently stowed in the hold, it has actively enriched our knowledge of ancient Phoenician shipbuilding. Furthermore, while the presence in the Cape Gelydonia wreck of *brushwood dunnage* used to line the hull permitted the author to propose a new and now widely accepted interpretation of 'Odysseus last task in building his boat',[164] the analysis of these wrecks and of their cargos, especially in light of our knowledge of the Iberic-Phoenician ships and boats, provides us with some important information about the use of these Phoenician ships 'which sank about the time of the Trojan War'.[165]

The wood remains found at Ulu Burun, which have been dated to 1305 BC, confirm that the use of the mortise-and-tenon joinery for the planking of hulls in use in the Mediterranean was introduced by Canaanite shipbuilders, presumably in the framework of the proto-Phoenician shipbuilding tradition. The architectural studies on this wreck demonstrate in fact that the ship, conceived as hull-based, was in fact built shell-first using cedar wood. The framing was probably absent rather than spaced out at distances of 'more than 1.80 meters', since the preserved portion of the hull, which comprises part of the keel, the two garboards, and at least two more planks on both sides, lack any evidence of frame-fixing stations. In addition, as Pulak (2003) has noted, some aspects of the joinery in use at Ulu Burun, such as the length of the tenons and their disposition, can be read as proof of some kind of hidden skeleton. Interestingly, the hull of the wreck from Cape Gelydonia shows the same structural features. Even though the low number of wooden fragments found still in connection initially prevented a proper identification of the technology of this ship,[166] the possibility of identifying some of the woods that were used in recovered elements of the joinery, made possible thanks to the finding of the woods used in the Ulu Burun wreck,[167] confirm the cultural-technical link between these two ships.

In terms of their load and usage, both these vessels seem to have been used to transport several objects from very mixed cargoes that originated from several harbours or ports-of-trade around the Mediterranean coast.[168] However, in both cases copper ingots were apparently

[162] Bass 1972: 22-24.

[163] Bass *and alii* 1985.

[164] 'Odysseus last task in building a boat was to spread over it a great deal of brushwood. Its purpose was seldom understood by modern translators of Homer before the discovery of [..] the Bronze Age Ship found near cape Gelydonia, Turkey. Fragmentary wooden members revealed that methods used in its construction was identical to those described by Homer' (Bass 1972: 24).

[165] Bass 1972: 24.

[166] Bass 1964.

[167] Bass 1994.

[168] According to Peyronnel 'the entire cargo found on-board the Ulu Burun vessel could have been stowed on-board the ship at a single harbour. However, we cannot exclude the possibility that it was built up during a journey with multiple stops' (Peyronnel 2008: 169).

predominant among the preserved objects, thus confirming the identification of these ships as Phoenician merchantmen, as proposed by Bass. As we have seen, between the end of the Bronze Age and the beginning of the Iron Age, metal trading was the main activity of the Phoenician navy. Moreover, the discovery of an ox-hide shaped mould made of calcar, at Ras Ibn Hani in Syria, seems to confirm a suggestion first raised in connection with the analysis of Egyptian iconography: namely that during the Late Bronze Age, ox-hide copper ingots were moved for the most part onboard Siro-Canaanite ships.[169]

Focusing more specifically on the Ulu Burun wreck and its particular load[170] raises some interesting points to note. Firstly, the route: there are a number of factors, like the presence of objects of the load coming from different places around the Mediterranean,[171] to suggest that the boat must have sailed from Canaan, 'maybe from Abu Hawam on the Israeli coast',[172] to Ugarit in northern Syria, and then on to Cyprus.[173] Unfortunately, we cannot know the name of the sailors, nor of the ship-owner. However, there are also several elements to suggest that this boat, of Levantine origin, was travelling 'on behalf of a Canaanite king [...] carrying a sort of gift',[174] and was sent to another prince, possibly of Mycenaean origin,[175] as it was in use at that time in the Levant. The high number of exotic objects that comprised the ship's load in fact recall 'the aristocratic trades of the Levant of the LBA',[176] when gifts among princes and kings of different reigns used to be moved onboard Levantine merchantmen.

These trades, originating in the second millennium BC, are depicted inside different Egyptian tombs.[177] This is particularly true of the tombs from the eighteenth dynasty, such as that of Kenamun of Thebe, in which Syrian ships are depicted approaching an Egyptian harbour with their precious loads.[178] These images are also described in some Akkadian and Ugaritic texts.

Dating some forty years after the wreckage of the ship of Uluburun, a clay tablet speaks about a similar ship, sent by Sinaranu, a local merchant,[179] from Ugarit to Crete. In this text, we read:[180]

> From this day on, Ammishtamru,
> son of Niqmepa, king of Ugarit,
> has exempted Sinaranu, son of Siginu;
> he is clear as the sun is clear.
> Neither his grain, nor his beer, nor his oil
> will enter the palace (as tribute).

[169] Peyronnel 2008: 169.
[170] Pulack 1997: 233-262; Wachsmann 1998: 303-7; Peyronnel 2008: 174-85, Cline 2014: 92-97; Cline E.H., Yasur-Landau A. 2007.
[171] Fitzgerald 1997: 431.
[172] Cline 2014: 92.
[173] Wahcsmann 1998: 306-07.
[174] Wachsmann 1998: 307; Cline 2014: 93.
[175] As Cline has pointed out, 'It is absolutely evident that the loss of this ship must have been a great loss for a man or a reign' (Cline 2014: 93).
[176] Peyronnel 2008: 183.
[177] Bass 1972: 23.
[178] Dinkel, Davies 1963: pl. XV; Vinson 1994: 40-41; Wachsmann 1998: 313-14; Peyronnel 2008: 183-85.
[179] From other Egyptian texts (Cline 2014: 97-98) we know that Sinaranu was a rich merchant from Ugarit who gained his wealth during the reign of Ammistarmu II, and who arranged a maritime expedition in 1250 BC.
[180] This is the translation proposed by Hoftijzer and Van Soldt (Wachsmann 1998: 340).

His ship is free (from claims).
If his ship comes (back) from Crete,
he will bring his present to the king
and herald will not come near his house.
Sinaranu is dedicated to the king, [....]
The [...] belongs to his sons' forever.[181]

Apart from the parallel drawn between the boat of Sinaranu and the wreck of Ulu Burun,[182] the most interesting aspect of this text is that it outlines how private merchants used to pay tributes to the palace by means of their merchant-ships, and how they could be exempted from this duty.[183] According to some scholars,[184] the analysis of other tablets permits to conclude that this should happen after certain key events, among which were included battles and expeditions.

As we have seen, the concept of paying tribute in the form of ships appears to have still been in the first millennium BC; this is demonstrated both in certain inscriptions and in the figures on the Balawat bronze bands, as well as on other Assyrian reliefs from the Early Iron Age. According to the archaeological evidence, both from the Bronze and the Early Iron Ages, tributes and princely gifts were composed largely from exotic objects, raw materials such as timbers or copper, and precious metals, primarily silver. With regard to princely gifts, another Ugaritic text,[185] dated to around the 1185 BC[186] is of particular interest. Here, we can read:[187]

List of People who have entered the palace of the King
and who have not been put in a document before:
Yarim'al the Tyrian, Irseyu,
Ya'ziraddu, Ayachu, Bin Ayaltu.
540 [shekel] is the silver of a ship that has entered
into a ship for the King of Byblos,
and the King of Byblos has taken 50 shekels of silver
for the outfitting of his ships in 'rm[188]
as the silver due for its payment.

From this text, we briefly learn how a ship of the king of Byblos — and thus a Phoenician Merchantman — was used to send a tribute to the king of Ugarit on behalf of five dignitaries, all of whom came from different cities and were of 'new acquisition' as tribute-bearers. The use of a single ship to bring tributes from several different bearers to the king of Ugarit is in

[181] Text: RS 16.238+254.
[182] Cline 2014: 97-98.
[183] In another similar text (RS 16.386), King Ammistarmu II frees 'Bin-yassuba and Bin?...and his sons forever, when coming back from their journeys to Egypt, to Hatti and to the land of Z[..] from the duty to refer to the officers of the Palace'.
[184] Peyronnel 2008: 135-58; Cline 2014: 97-98.
[185] Text: KTU 4.338.
[186] Wachsmann 1998: 334.
[187] Hoftijzer, Van Soldt 1998: 337-38.
[188] 'rm indicated a locality in the Reign of Ugarit (Hofijtzer, Van Soldt 1998: 338).

fact attested in other texts. In one such entry,[189] which reports on the wreckage and loss of a cargo of copper, we read:[190]

> Hundred ten/twenty...copper is lost in a ship
> 20 for the people from Umd
> 10 for Kutilana.

On the other hand, it is clear that ships were also borrowed for use in trading and tribute bearing, as suggested by two different texts from Ugarit. In the first of these texts, a tablet found at the palace,[191] we find a list of ships stationed at the main harbour of the kingdom, Mahadu: some of these names must reflect local tradition, while other names reflect other cities and cultures.[192]

> The ships from Mahadu
> The br-vessel of Tipatbaal
> The br-vessel of dmty
> The tkt-vessel of Tarraiyanu,
> The br.vessel of Abdimilku...

From a nautical perspective, from this short list, although it is unfortunately damaged, we can recognize two different types of vessel: the *br-vessel*, possibly of local origin, and used to trade and to fight on the sea; and the *tkt-vessel*.[193] With regards to the latter, it should be noted that some four centuries after this Ugaritic text was written, we find a direct reference to this class of vessel in the biblical book of Isaiah:[194] here, in Isaiah 2,16, the tkt-vessel is described as 'a ship from Tarsis'. Written in the eighth century BC, the book of Isaiah speaks of the Levant of the Early Iron Age, when Tarsis, a Syrian city on the eastern Mediterranean coast, was used as harbour by the Phoenicians who traded metals across the whole Mediterranean basin.[195]

Each of these elements pertaining to ancient ships and wrecks, when combined, make it possible to trace some kind of evolutionary line that links the hulls of the Late Bronze Age to those of the Early Iron Age at a time when the cargo, the seamen, the routes, and the purposes of seafaring showed very little variation. The proposition first put forward by Bass in the early 1970s, when he spoke about the wreck of Cape Gelydonia, has in fact found its archaeological dimension through these data, which permitted Casson to state:

> The Phoenicians went in for hulls that were broad of beam and rounded at both stem and stern, and usually garnished with a horse's head as adornment for the prow. Greek writers dubbed such craft either gauloi ('tubs') because of their shape or hippoi ('horses') because of the figurehead.[196]

[189] Text: KTU 4.394.
[190] Hoftijzer, Van Soldt 1998: 339.
[191] Text: KTU 4.81.
[192] Hoftijzer, Van Soldt 1998: 337.
[193] Hoftijzer, Van Soldt 1998: 337.
[194] Lipinksi 1971: 87.
[195] Bernardini 2014: 39.
[196] Casson 1994: 41.

The ἵππος ship and the Trojan War

Despite the rich archaeological record pertaining to the different phases of the citadel that was discovered on Hassarlik Mountain, the identification of Ilion remains doubtful.[197] However, we cannot ignore the fact that the excavated site has provided significant information about the role it played in the control of the Dardanelles, the key waterway to the Black Sea, and its mines, which might have proved an important focus in the Trojan War as it is narrated by Homer.[198] As has been noted by several authors, the growth and subsequent fall of the site of (the presumed) Ilion must be examined 'in the light of the difficult system of relationships involving the Hittite reign and the Mycenaean world between the 15th and the 12th centuries BC'.[199] As we have seen in this chapter, these relationships included the payment of tribute, the granting of princely gifts, and war.[200]

According to Akkadian[201] and Ugaritic texts,[202] from at least the late third millennium BC, the goods and the raw materials involved in these practices used to be sailed overseas onboard merchantmen for the purposes of trading among the different reigns of the Mediterranean Basin. The Levantine origin of the merchant-ships that were employed for such traffic appears to be confirmed by their identification as of Siro-Canaanite origin or production. In addition, and thanks to some of the tablets that were found in the archives of the Assyrian palaces, we are aware that most of the craftsmen working in the shipyards of the Levant during the second millennium BC were of Siro-Canaanite origin and that the majority of the wood-types used in local shipbuilding came from the Phoenician harbours of the Levant.[203]

From a naval perspective, the link between the Siro-Canaanite and the Phoenician maritime culture appears evident,[204] as it indeed was for the cultures of these two civilizations. As Paolo Bernardini has noted, based on the archaeological evidence, we can reasonably conclude that during the last quarter of the second millennium BC, 'the main coastal cities of the Canaanite region become Phoenician because they remain themselves. While everything changes, they remain Canaanite',[205] with the Phoenicians adopting the social and political structures of the ancient Canaanites.

In the first centuries of the first millennium BC, there are a number of elements that allow us to conclude that the use of merchant ships of Phoenician origin for bearing tribute overseas to the kings of the eastern Mediterranean remained an active tradition. It is no coincidence that the bronze bands of Balawat depict some ἵππος ships loading and unloading their cargoes of precious metals for presentation to the Assyrian kings. As such, even though we cannot know for certain whether the Trojan War, as it is presented in the poems narrated by Homer, took place during the Late Bronze Age or in the Early Iron Age, [206] we can nonetheless affirm

[197] Cultraro 2004: 207.
[198] Baldacci 2017: 5.
[199] Cultraro 2004: 211.
[200] Peyronnel 2008: 139-158.
[201] Baldacci 2017: 12-20.
[202] Hoftijzer, Van Soldt 1998: 333-43.
[203] Baldacci 2017: 5-27.
[204] Casson 1971: 35-38; Wachsmann 1998: 39-60.
[205] Bernardini 2014: 9.
[206] As many authors have commented, there are a number of textual elements, pertaining in particular to maritime culture, in the *Iliad* and the *Odyssey* (Mark 2005) that appear to refer to the first quarter of the first millennium BC.

that the use of Phoenician merchantmen had spread as far as the area where the war took place and would have been active, regardless of its precise date. Known as either *gauloi* or *hippoi* by the Greeks,[207] these merchant-vessels appear to have been well known by Homer: it is unsurprising that the Greek poet can reasonably be considered as the first author to write about these ships in ancient times. When describing the boats of Mentes, for example, he informs us that they were fast, agile, round, decked, and powered by a mixture of sail and oars.[208] He thus provides us with many details about these hulls, which have only recently been confirmed by analysis both of ancient naval iconography and of the wrecks pertaining to this class of ship.[209] In addition, there is reasonable evidence to suggest that in the episode of the presumed 'wooden horse' of Troy, Homer was in fact referring to the construction of one of these decked hulls, conceived as a merchantmen and usually used to bear tribute to kings after a defeat, rather than to the fabrication of a great wooden statue shaped like a horse, as a way to bring an end to the siege of Troy.

[207] Casson 1994: 41.

[208] Homer, *Odyssey* II.385-434.

[209] Homer's description is a good fit for those ships depicted on the Balawat Gates and at Khorsabad: round merchantmen, which were moved by both oars and sails, and which transported metal objects and precious woods. Furthermore, according to excavations at the site (Pomey 2012), the analysis of the Golo wreck seem to confirm what we know from ancient sources about the presence of a deck on the hulls of boats of Phoenician origin in the EIA.

Why Homer Never Talked About a Horse

Much knowledge and memory of the Trojan War must initially have circulated in oral tradition, and all these events were first set down in writing before the end of the eight century BC.[1] That was the time when 'the Greeks of the Homeland had learned to write again, a product of their renewed relations with the Near East'.[2] We do not know whether this war took place for real, or if its narration is to read as a sort of founding myth for the new-born Greek ethnos: whatever the truth, our knowledge of the events lacks any strictly historical detail. The new-born Greek society of the Early Iron Age seems to look for her glorious ancestors by turning to the Bronze Age, celebrating the competition with the other eastern actors for the control of the eastern routes of the Mediterranean.

However, Achaean princes and rulers that moved to the Trojan shores at the beginning of the Iliad anticipate and recall the mythic Trojan heroes that sailed the Mediterranean after the war, founding many of the colonies of the west,[3] and the active role played in the Trojan War by the deities, both for the Greeks and for the Trojans, seems to support the interpretation of Homer's narrations as a sort of 'sacred book'.

With regards to the events that inspired the bard, we can be reasonably certain that some kind of Greek military activity occurred in north-western Anatolia during the Late Bronze Age,[4] and that this in all likelihood involved some pre-Greek actors. However, as stated above, the long-lasting siege of the city of Troy as described in the Iliad falls more closely within the war culture of the Levantine area for the Bronze Age.[5]

As seen above, even though the Trojan War cannot be considered a proper naval war, the link between Homer's narratives and the importance of the role played by the sea for the creation of the Greek cultures of the Early Iron Age as a direct descendant from the Minoan and Mycenaean glorious past is evident, starting at least from the Book Two of the Iliad. Between 1600 and 1100 BC, the presence of several types of ship, all similar but nonetheless featuring some variation, seems to reflect the idea of the existence of 'several Mycenaean fleets [...] properties of different princes [...] of which the Homeric Catalogue of Ships may represents a reliable reflection'.[6]

As a number of scholars have stated,[7] the Homeric epics, nowadays considered an important primary source for our knowledge of the ancient ships, reflected the naval dimension of the Greek culture of the Early Iron Age: Homeric audience was confronted with a system of nautical terminology, surprisingly developed and closed to us but easily understandable to them, shared with the author.[8]

---

1 Rossi 1977; Hedreen 1995: 153; Reber 2007: 25.
2 Boardman 2014: 25.
3 Guzzo 2011; Pomey 1996.
4 Cline 2018: 25-34; Janni 1994: 7; Boardman 2014: 25; Baldacci 2017: 27.
5 Liverani 2017: 123.
6 Basch 1987: 156
7 Morrison, Williams 1968: 43-69; Kurt 1979; Basch 1987: 157-58; Mc Grail 2000: 126-28.
8 Kurt 1979: 219.

It is with this awareness of this background knowledge about ships and seafaring that both Homer and his audience would have brought to the narrative that we can nowadays propose, reading the single account by Homer of the last night of Tory in its proper naval dimension. Furthermore, what discussed in the previous chapters, allows us proposing a new reading for the 'Wooden Horse of Troy which Epeius made with Athena's help' (*ἵππου δουρατέου, τὸν Ἐπειὸς ἐποίησεν σὺν Ἀθήνῃ*) as described by Homer in the Odyssey.[9] The 'contrivance' (*μηχάνημα*) used by the Acheans to conquer Troy, and reported by Pausanias in his Description of Greece,[10] was not a simulacre of a big horse, it was indeed one of the ships 'broad of beam and rounded at both stem and stern [...] garnished with a horse's head as adornment for the prow [that the] 'Greek writers dubbed *Hippoi* ('horses') because of the figurehead'.[11]

Homer's words in their proper context

Despite a great number of ancient authors like Pausanias, Euphorion of Calchis, Johannes Lydus, Pliny the Elder,[12] did not accept the idea that what described by Homer could have been a horse, all the modern-day translators of the *Odyssey* invariably understand the author's words as being the first actual description of the giant simulacre of a wooden horse, created with divine assistance. However, focusing on Homer's words, and the war background they refer to, it is by no means impossible that the original narration was imbued with a precise meaning to its specific audience, perfectly aware of the maritime dimension of the Early Iron Age.[13]

The naval perspective of the description of the ἵππος as made by Homer appears evident because of the use of the word δουρατέος, which meaning is not, as usually indicated by modern-day translators, 'made of wood', but, as discussed above, 'made of planks' in the sense of 'the planks of the bulwark of a hull'. Homer himself confirms this interpretation of the term, as we can learn by reading other passages of both the Iliad and the Odysssey. [14] All these passages testify for how the word δουρατέος must be directly linked to the word δούρατα 'planks', rather than to the word δουρος, 'wood, or tree'.

Homeric epics record that the deception was not conceived by Odysseys, as reported many centuries later, between the 3rd and the 5th century CE, by Quintus of Smyrna, and sometimes still accepted.

> ὣς ἄρ' ἔφη: τῶν δ' οὔτις ἔφη φρεσὶ τεκμήρασθαι
> ἄλκαρ ὀϊζυροῖο μόθου: δίζοντο δὲ μῆχος
> εὑρέμεναι: μοῦνος δὲ σαοφροσύνῃσι νόησεν
> υἱὸς Λαέρταο καὶ ἀντίον ἔκφατο μῦθον:
> 'ὦ φίλ', ἐπουρανίοισι τετιμένε πάγχυ θεοῖσιν,

---

[9] Homer, *Odyssey* VIII.491-92.

[10] Pausanias, *Description of Greece* I.23.8

[11] Casson 1994: 41.

[12] See above Chapter 2 and 3.

[13] It is to point out that LBA – EIA naval traditions of the eastern Mediterranean region show several connections, and a sort of long-lasting technological stability for what concern the forms and dimensions of the hull, the ship-types in use, and the shipbuilding technology (Pomey, Kahanov, Rieth 2012; Pomey. Rieth 2005; McGrail 2000; Pomey 1997; Casson 1971).

[14] Homer, *Iliad*, VII; *Odyssey*, V.162; V.370; V.371.

εἰ ἐτεὸν πέπρωται ἐϋπτολέμοισιν Ἀχαιοῖς
ἐκπέρσαι Πριάμοιο δολοφροσύνῃσι πόληα,
ἵππον τεκτήναντες ἀριστέες ἐς λόχον ἄνδρες
βησόμεθ' ἀσπασίως:

He spoke; but no man's wit might find a way
To escape their grievous travail as they sought
To find a remedy, till Laertes' son
Discerned it of his wisdom, and he spoke:
" Friend, in high honour held of the Heavenly Ones,
If doomed it be indeed that Priam's burg by guile must fall
before the war-worn Greeks, A great Horse let us fashion,
in the which Our mightiest shall take ambush. [15]

As seen above, in thc Homeric epics the ἵππος was in fact built by Epeius under Athena Pallas' rules and with her divine help.[16]

The link between Athena and Epeius seems to be confirmed in its maritime dimension through post-Homeric mythology. On his journey back from Troy, Epeius is said to have sailed on the sea to Southern Italy, and landed in the Gulf of Taranto, where he founded the colony of Metapontum, or Lagaria, in the place in which he devoted to Athena the tools that he used for the construction of the ἵππος.[17]

Regarding Athena, for the Greeks, the deity was the protector of the craftsmen and, particularly when identified as Pallas, she was also the protector of the shipwrights. This characteristic appears to be primarily linked to the construction of the Argo ship, as reported in the Argonautica written by Apollonius of Rhodes in the 3rd century BC.

νῆα μὲν οὖν οἱ πρόσθεν ἐπικλείουσιν ἀοιδοὶ
Ἄργον Ἀθηναίης καμέειν ὑποθημοσύνῃσιν.

Now minstrels even before my day do tell
how Argus by the counsels of Athena build a ship for him[18]

αὐτή μιν Τριτωνὶς ἀριστήων ἐς ὅμιλον
ὦρσεν Ἀθηναίη, μετὰ δ' ἤλυθεν ἐλδομένοισιν.
αὐτὴ γὰρ καὶ νῆα θοὴν κάμε: σὺν δέ οἱ Ἄργος
τεῦξεν Ἀρεστορίδης κείνης ὑποθημοσύνῃσιν.

Him did Tritonian Athena herself rouse to the gathering of the chiefs,
and he came amongst men eager for his coming;
for it was Athena too, that builded the swift ship, and with her had Argus,

---

[15] Quinto Smirneo, *Posthomerica* XII.21-29.
[16] Homer, *Odyssey* IV.492-94; XI.523-35. As noted by Cline (2015: 19) 'this attribution is followed also by Lesches, in the VII century BC', when writing is poem, part of the Epic Cycle.
[17] Grimal 1990: 212.
[18] Apollonius of Rhodes, *Argonautica* I.18-19. (Translated by E.P. Coleridge 1889)

son of Arestor, fashioned it by her counsels.[19]

τὴν γὰρ Ἀθηναίη τεχνήσατο, καὶ τάμε χαλκῷ
δούρατα Πηλιάδος κορυφῆς πέρι: σὺν δέ οἱ Ἄργος
τεῦξεν. [...]

For it was Athena that built this ship and cut with brazen axe
Her planks about the peak of Pelion: and with the goddess
Worked Argus.[20]

In this description of Athena guiding Argos during the construction of the ship, we can easily find interesting parallel with what stated by Homer in the Odyssey,[21] and Homer himself attests to the relationship between Athena and shipwrights by referring to her persuasion of Zeus to send his messenger to Calypso to make Odysseus build his raft;[22] and her involvement in convincing the Phaeacians to provide Odysseus with a ship for his journey back.[23]

Further, in the *Odyssey*, the bard attests to the existence of a close relationship between Athena and those merchantmen that the Greek dubbed ἵππος, with the deity invitation to Telemachus to embark on the ἵπποι of the Taphians.[24] Speaking of these ships, in fact, Homer describes through the voice of Penelope the merchantmen used by this non-Greek people to trade metal[25] and names them 'the ἵπποι of the sea' ('αἵ θ'ἁλὸς ἵπποι ἀνδράσι γίγνονται').[26]

Additional supports to the naval interpretation for what built by Epeius comes from the synonyms used by Homer himself when referring to the ἵππος in his epics, among which we list κοῖλον λόχον 'concave hideout',[27] and κοῖλον δόρυ 'concave wood'.[28]

In ancient Greek texts the word κοῖλον is in fact primarily used to indicate the hold of the ships[29] or, when used in the plural, τα κοῖλα, the 'ships' themselves.[30] Even the word δόρυ is often used to define a ship when used in a metaphorical sense, both in association with the word ναῦς, as seen in different parts of the Odyssey, or on its own.[31] We can also point out that, in Greek mythology, the term alone describe the Argo ship built by Argo under Athena's help.

---

[19] Apollonius of Rhodes, *Argonautica* I.109-112. (Translated by E.P. Coleridge 1889)

[20] Apollonius of Rhodes, Argonautica II.1184-1189.

[21] According to what narrated in the Argonautica, at the time of the expedition 'the art of navigation had not yet been invented' (Grimal 1990: 61), therefore Athena needed to guide Argo in the construction of the ship. As for Argo, also for Epeius Athena acted like a guide, we know in fact, that no passages, nor in the Iliad and in the Odyssey, attribute to Epeius any specific ability as a blacksmith, carpenter, or shipwright: the hero could build the ἵππος only thanks to Athena's help.

[22] Homer, *Odyssey* V.5-20.

[23] Homer, *Odyssey* VIII.8 -23.

[24] Homer, Odyssey I.105-318.

[25] As stated by Sherrat, the Iliad testify for how, in EIA Greece, 'the name Phoenicians applied on the basis of the maritime activities (of trading). [...] In this sense, it could as well have applied to any East Mediterranean mariner" (Sherrat 2010b: 124).

[26] Homer, *Odyssey* IV.708-709.

[27] Homer, *Odyssey* IV.277.

[28] Homer, *Odyssey* IV.507.

[29] Theocritus, *Idyllis* 22.12; Athaeneus, *fragment* 206,

[30] Appian, *The Civil Wars* V.

[31] Sophocles, *Thrachiniae*.

[32] Lastly, the terms used by Homer to describe the actions that involved the horse also refer to the naval sphere, particularly the verb ἐρύσαντο[33] that indicate the launching and hauling of ships.[34]

The deception planned by Athena Pallas

As far as Athena Pallas' involvement in the episode that ends the Trojan siege, the active role played by the deity appears to be linked not only to her naval dimension, but also to the presence of the temple on the top of the citadel of Troy. There are two main reasons why that make this element fundamental to the success of the Achaean deception, as the temple was dedicated to Pallas – that is, to Athena Pallas.

Since the Trojan war was a siege unfolded in accordance with the rules of the war culture of the Levant, the patron goddess of the Trojans, a Levantine people, must have surely been aware of those rules, among which, as we have seen above, there was that of the payment of a tribute to the winner at the end of the siege. Several sources, both iconographic and written, provide us with information about this practice as well as about the use of merchant-ships to pay these tributes, at least from the Bronze Age and up to the 8th century BC.[35]

From the Bronze Age on, tributes carried on board of these ships were mainly composed from exotic objects, copper, and precious metals, and the concept of paying tribute in the form of ships appears to have still been in the first millennium BC, as we can see through certain inscriptions and figures like those on the Balawat bronze bands and other Assyrian reliefs[36]. The bronze bands of Balawat depict some *ἵπποι* ships landed on a beach, hauled thanks to some ropes tied around the horsehead-figurehead's neck to the wall, and then unloading their cargoes of precious metals for presentation to the Assyrian kings.

Homeric epics suggest that Athena's plan was based on faking the defeat: this was in fact the only way the Achaeans had for making the Trojans opening the walls of the citadel. Therefore, we can argue that the best way for pretending the defeat of this war for the control of the Dardanelles, the key waterway to the Black Sea, and its mines,[37] was acting like a defeated army. That meant paying the tribute to the winner or, saying it with Muscarella, 'giving the King what he wanted and expected'.[38]

Following the war customs of that time, this could be done by bearing exotic objects and precious metals, carried on a 'ἵππος' ship, next to the wall of the citadel. As the bronze bands of the Balawat gates show, the ship should have been hauled inside the citadel by the Trojans themselves, in order to bring the precious metal to the palace or to some other sacred site, particularly to the temple of the patron god.[39]

[32] Euphorion, *Andromachas* 793
[33] Homer, *Odyssey* V.371.
[34] Homer, *Iliad* IV.248; XIV.30, 75; XVIII.69; *Odyssey*, IV.666: 780; X.403; XI.2.
[35] Muscarella 1998.
[36] See Chapter 5.
[37] Baldacci 2017: 5; Cultraro 2006: 206-11.
[38] Muscarella 1998: 156.
[39] According to ancient texts from Akkad, precious metal could in fact be stored also in the temple or in tombs (Baldacci 2017: 104).

According to ancient texts, in fact, Levantine kings were not proprietors of their lands and reigns, 'but merely the stewards appointed by their divine owners' and 'their stewardship found its practical expressions in their office as chiefs of the priests of the deity'.[40] Thus, when receiving tribute in precious metals from enemies at the end of military campaigns, 'members of the Military were allowed to retain some of this treasure for them-selves, but the lion's share went to the king',[41] who administrated it on behalf and for the benefits of the gods.[42] Administration of tributes included the storage of precious metals in the palace and the temple: at Troy, this meant bringing them inside the wall of the citadel, and taking them up to the Pallas' temple.

Hauling a merchant-ship from a beach was a more common practice than we think. As noted by David Blackman, in fact, 'it is worth remarking [...] that though ancients merchant-ships were not shipped in Shipsheds, they certainly were beached [...] and we must allow for light timbers structures on the shores of commercial harbours [and] on any beach site that was used'.[43] Attested at least since the 3rd millennium BC[44], the hauling of beached ships were common in ancient times, as it just needed the opening of one of the doors of the citadel and building a light timber structure for hauling by implementing pulleys and rollers.

Evidence from tow slipways at Sounion, dating back to the fifth century BC, and referring to a ship-shed for small ship and with a gradient of 1 to 3.5,[45] permit Casson stating that, at Sounion, 'seacrafts were necessarily drawn up with the aid of winches and the like'.[46] Further evidence of what seems to be the mountings of three capstans come from Thurii, at the back of the pair of slipways which are fifth century or later,[47] and there is no doubt that more complex systems have existed in Greece and out of the Greek world during the first millennium BC.[48]

Notably, for what concern Troy, the hauling of the ἵππος' ship from the beach has been first suggested by Homer himself by stating

> αὐτοὶ γάρ μιν Τρῶες ἐς ἀκρόπολιν ἐρύσαντο
>
> *for the Trojans had themselves dragged it to the citadel.*[49]

Some centuries later, the operation entered the Vergil's description of the last night of Troy:

> Accingunt omnes operi pedibusque rotarum
> Subiciunt lapsus, et stuppea vincula collo
> Intendunt[...]

[40] Beckman 1995: 530.
[41] Beckman 1995: 538-39.
[42] As noted by Beckman, in Bronze Age Anatolia 'the king stood at the point of contact between the sphere of the gods and that of the humans [...] and the gods were thought to be literally dependent on the toil of their human servants' (Beckman 1995: 530).
[43] Blackman 1990: 45
[44] In a text from the Reign of Ur III, dated to the 2112-2104, we can read 'gis-us-ma-du' that means 'wooden sheds to haul and launch the ship' (Baldacci 2017: 103).
[45] Blackman 1990: 37.
[46] Casson 1971: 364.
[47] Blackman 1982: 205.
[48] Blackman 1990: 37-39.
[49] Homer, *Odyssey* IV.502-507

Everybody helps to put rollers under the machine
And to tie ropes around its neck.[50]

Turning to ancient texts, these short descriptions recall the use of complex hauling system as attested in the launch Hiero's great ship, the *Syracusia* directed by Archimedes reported by Athaeneus

> τὸ μὲν οὖν ἥμισυ τοῦ παντὸς τῆς νεὼς ἐν μησὶν ἓξ ξειργάσατο ... καὶ ταῖς ἐκ μολίβου ποιηθείσαις κεραμίσιν ἀεὶ καθ' ὃ ναυπηγηθείη μέρος περιελαμβάνετο, ὡς ἂν τριακοσίων ὄντων τῶν τὴν ὕλην ἐργαζομένων τεχνιτῶν χωρὶς τῶν ὑπηρετούντων. τοῦτο μὲν οὖν τὸ μέρος εἰς τὴν θάλασσαν καθέλκειν προσετέτακτο, τὴν λοιπὴν κατασκευὴν ἵν' ἐκεῖ λαμβάνῃ. ὡς δὲ περὶ τὸν καθελκυσμὸν αὐτοῦ τὸν εἰς τὴν θάλασσαν πολλὴ ζήτησις ἦν, Ἀρχιμήδης ὁ μηχανικὸς μόνος αὐτὸ κατήγαγε δι' ὀλίγων σωμάτων. κατασκευάσας γὰρ ἕλικα τὸ τηλικοῦτον σκάφος εἰς τὴν θάλασσαν κατήγαγε. πρῶτος δ' Ἀρχιμήδης εὗρε τὴν τῆς ἕλικος κατασκευήν. ὡς δὲ καὶ τὰ λοιπὰ μέρη τῆς νεὼς ἐν ἄλλοις ἓξ μησὶ κατεσκευάσθηκαὶ τοῖς χαλκοῖς ἥλοιςπᾶσα περιελήφθη, ὧν οἱ πολλοὶ δεκάμνοοι ἦσαν, οἱ δ' ἄλλοι τούτων ἡμιόλιοι —διὰ τρυπάνων δ' ἦσαν οὗτοι ἡρμοσμένοι τοὺς σταμῖνας συνέχοντες· μολυβδίναις δὲ κεραμίσιν ἐπεστεγνοῦντο πρὸς τὸ ξύλον, ὑποτιθεμένων ὀθονίων μετὰ πίττης —ὡς οὖν τὴν ἐκτὸς ἐπιφάνειαν ἐξειργάσατο, τὴν ἐντὸς διασκευὴν ἐξεπονεῖτο.
>
> One half, then, of the entire ship he finished in six months. . . and as each part of the ship was completed it was overlaid with tiling made of lead; for there were about three hundred artisans working on the materials, not including their assistants. This part of the ship, then, was ordered to be launched in the sea, that it might receive the finishing touches there. But after considerable discussion in regard to the method of pulling it into the water, Archimedes the mechanician alone was able to launch it with the help of a few persons. For by the construction of a windlass he was able to launch a ship of so great proportions in the water. Archimedes was the first to invent the construction of the windlass. The remaining parts of the ship were completed in another period of six months; it was entirely secured with bronze rivets, most of which weighed ten pounds, while the rest were half as large again; these wit were fitted in place by means of augers, and held the stanchions together; fixed to the timbers was a sheath of leaden tiles, under which were strips of linen canvas covered with pitch. When, then, he had completed the outside surface, he proceeded to make complete the inner arrangements.[51]

and confirmed by Plutarch:

> θαυμάσαντος δὲ τοῦ Ἱέρωνος, καὶ δεηθέντος εἰς ἔργον ἐξαγαγεῖν τὸ πρόβλημα καὶ δεῖξαί τι τῶν μεγάλων κινούμενον ὑπὸ σμικρᾶς δυνάμεως, ὁλκάδα τριάρμενον τῶν βασιλικῶν πόνῳ μεγάλῳ καὶ χειρὶ πολλῇ νεωλκηθεῖσαν, ἐμβαλὼν ἀνθρώπους τε πολλοὺς καὶ τὸν συνήθη φόρτον, αὐτὸς ἄπωθεν καθήμενος, οὐ μετὰ σπουδῆς ἀλλ' ἠρέμα τῇ χειρὶ σείων ἀρχήν τινα πολυσπάστου, προσηγάγετο, λείως καὶ ἀπταίστως ὥσπερ διὰ θαλάσσης ἐπιθέουσαν.

[50] Vergil, *Aeneid* II.235-237
[51] Athenaeus, *The Deipnosophists* V.207 a-b.

> Hiero was astonished, and begged him to put his proposition into execution, and show him some great weight moved by a slight force. Archimedes therefore fixed upon a three-masted merchantman of the royal fleet, which had been dragged ashore by the great labours of many men, and after putting on board many passengers and the customary freight, he seated himself at a distance from her, and without any great effort, but quietly setting in motion with his hand a system of compound pulleys, drew her towards him smoothly and evenly, as though she were gliding through the water.[52]

Both these texts testify for how the Greek inventor used a multiple block and tackle for the purpose of hauling the big ship.[53]

The roman poet Horace too refers to a machine used for hauling ships after their storage in land down to the water in spring

> Soluitur acris hiems grata vice veris et Favoni
> trahuntque siccas machinae carinas
>
> Spring, and the bitter winter thaws as west winds warm the earth,
> and boats are dragged from storage to the shore.[54]

Further, in his *De Architectura* Vitruvius describes arrangements of blocks and tackle in use in Roman time, for hauling ships ashore

> Sumuntur tigna amplissima longitudine; supra figuntur chelonia, in quibus cluduntur suculae. Per media autem spatia tignorum insecantur exciduntur formae, in quibus excisionibus cluduntur capitula catapultarum, cuneisque distinentur, ne in contentionibus moveantur. Tum vero modioli aerei in ea capitula includuntur et in eos cuneoli ferrei, quas epizygidas Graeci vocant, conlocantur.
>
> Deinde ansae rudentum induntur per foramina capitulorum, in alteram partem traiciuntur, deinde in suculas coiciuntur involvuntur, uti vectibus per eas ext<enti> rudentes, cum manibus sunt tacti, aequalem in utroque sonitus habeant in responsum. Tunc autem cuneis ad foramina concluduntur, ut non possint se remittere. Ita traiecti in alteram partem eadem ratione vectibus per suculas extenduntur, donec aequaliter sonent. Ita cuneorum conclusionibus ad sonitum musicis auditionibus catapultae temperantur.
>
> Beams of very generous length are selected, and upon them are nailed socket-pieces in which windlasses are inserted. Midway along their length the beams are incised and cut away to form framings, and in these cuttings the capitals of the catapults are inserted, and prevented by wedges from moving when the stretching is going on. Then the bronze boxes are inserted into the capitals, and the little iron bolts, which the Greeks call ἐπιζυγίδες are put in their places in the boxes.

[52] Plutarch, *Parallel Lives. Marcellus* XIV.8.
[53] Casson 1971: 194-95; Blackman 1990: 37.
[54] Horace, *Odes* I.4.2

> Next, the loops of the strings are put through the holes in the capitals, and passed through to the other side; next, they are put upon the windlasses, and wound round them in order that the strings, stretched out taut on them by means of the handspikes, on being struck by the hand, may respond with the same sound on both sides. Then they are wedged tightly into the holes so that they cannot slacken. So, in the same manner, they are passed through to the other side, and stretched taut on the windlasses by means of the handspikes until they give the same sound. Thus with tight wedging, catapults are tuned to the proper pitch by musical sense of hearing.[55]

As David Blackman notes 'we may have references to hauling equipment as early as Herodotus'

> Παυσάμενος δὲ τῆς διώρυχος ὁ Νεκῶς ἐτράπετο πρὸς στρατηίας, καὶ τριήρεες αἱ μὲν ἐπὶ τῇ βορηίῃ θαλάσσῃ ἐποιήθησαν, αἱ δ' ἐν τῷ Ἀραβίῳ κόλπῳ ἐπὶ τῇ Ἐρυθρῇ θαλάσσῃ, τῶν ἔτι οἱ ὁλκοὶ ἐπίδηλοι.
>
> Necos, then, stopped work on the canal and engaged in preparations for war; some of his ships of war were built on the northern sea, and some in theArabian Gulf, by the Red Sea coast: the winches for landing these can still be seen.[56]
>
> *Ἐξ ὧν δὲ ἐξανέστησαν χώρων ἐν τούτοισι δὴ οἵ τε ὁλκοὶ τῶν νεῶν καὶ τὰ ἐρείπια τῶν οἰκημάτων τὸ μέχρις ἐμέο ἦσαν*
>
> There still remained in my day, in the places out of which the Ionians and Carians were turned, the winches for their ships and the ruins of their houses. [57]

Written about mid fifth century BC, these texts speak of the installations, still visible when the Greek historians visited Egypt, built on the Red Sea for his triremes by the Pharaoh Necho, who died 593 BC, and by Greeks at a garrison post in the eastern Nile Delta at the same period.[58] In both these passages, the Greek historian uses the word ὅλκοι to indicate the device in use for hauling. Normally translated by modern-days translators as whintches, as noted by David Blackman this word is indeed to interpret as 'hauling equipment'.

In fact, in the fifth century BC, Thucydides, the Greek historian considered the father of *scientific-history*, uses the same word ὁλκοὶ of equipment for hauling ships across the isthmus at Corinth.

> Τοιαῦτα μὲν οἱ Μυτιληναῖοι εἶπον. οἱ δὲ Λακεδαιμόνιοι καὶ οἱ ξύμμαχοι ἐπειδὴ ἤκουσαν, προσδεξάμενοι τοὺς λόγους ξυμμάχους τε τοὺς Λεσβίους ἐποιήσαντο, καὶ τὴν ἐς τὴν Ἀττικὴν ἐσβολὴν τοῖς τε ξυμμάχοις παροῦσι κατὰ τάχος ἔφραζον ἰέναι ἐς τὸν Ἰσθμὸν τοῖς δύο μέρεσιν ὡς ποιησόμενοι, καὶ αὐτοὶ πρῶτοι ἀφίκοντο, καὶ ὁλκοὺς παρεσκεύαζον τῶν νεῶν ἐν τῷ Ἰσθμῷ ὡς ὑπεροίσοντες ἐκ τῆς Κορίνθου ἐς τὴν πρὸς Ἀθήνας θάλασσαν καὶ ναυσὶ καὶ πεζῷ ἅμα ἐπιόντες.

[55] Vitruvius, *De Architectura* X.12.1-2
[56] Herodotus, *Histories* II.159.1.
[57] Herodotus, *Histories* II.154.5.
[58] Blackman 1990: 38.

> Such were the words of the Mitylenians. After hearing them out, the Lacedaemonians and confederates granted what they urged, and took the Lesbians into alliance, and deciding in favour of the invasion of Attica, told the allies present to march as quickly as possible to the Isthmus with two-thirds of their forces; and arriving there first themselves, got ready hauling machines to carry their ships across from Corinth to the sea on the side of Athens, in order to make their attack by sea and land at once. [59]

Turning back to our crucial episode, these texts permit us stating that opening the door of Tory did not mean for the Trojans opening the door leaves: hauling an ἵππος' ship, with her high figureheads carved ahead and abaft, needed the arrangement of a complex system which include the removal of the architrave. Vergil's description of the episode seems to confirm this removal of the architrave of the door of the city, and this may be the reason way the Latin poet writes:

> Dividimus muros, et moenia pandimus urbis
>
> We separate the walls and remove the defence of the city.[60]

Thus, as we can easily argue, once opened the door of the citadel could not be closed in a hurry: by accepting the gift, after a ten years long lasting siege, the Trojans finally removed the defence to their City.

Turning back to Athena's plan, the presence of warriors and heroes, with their armours and weapons, hided inside the hold of the ἵππος' ship was also a part of the goddess' plan. Aware of the presence of precious metals and exotic objects stowed in the hold as tribute, the Trojans would not be worried about the noises coming from the inside of the ship while moving on the rollers.

Further, as the king would not be directly involved in hauling operations, no-one would have had the opportunity to open the ports on the bulwarks before the ship had entered the citadel, and had reached the palace of the king or, at least, the dignitaries.

Therefore, once entered the citadel, the heroes who were onboard of the ἵππος' ship could easily reach their goal. It did not matter how many of them should have been hided inside the hull for real, they just had to kick-off the Achaean invasion of the citadel by giving the signal to those waiting aside from Trojans sight, and start fighting the Trojans inside the walls of their own City.

Finally, thanks to Athena Pallas' plan, the siege came to an end.

Two more elements must be highlighted. The use of a Ship of *Phoenician* origin, a ἵππος ship, makes sense because, as seen above, Levantine ships were often borrowed for use in trading and tribute bearing, as suggested by different texts from Ugarit. This practice was still in use in the eighth century BC, when a *tkt-vessel* of Ugatiric memory, and Phoenician origin, appears

[59] Thucydides, *Peloponnesian War* III.15.1.
[60] Vergil, *Aeneid* II.234.

in the biblical book of Isahia (II, 16) presented as '*a ship from Tarsis*'.[61] Further, as the Achaeans reached the Trojan shores coming from different isles and reigns, the use of a levantine ship, known by the People of the Eastern Mediterranean Sea as the ship in use for metals trading, permits the Greeks pretending their surrender 'as Achaeans as a People', avoiding the risk to identify any single prince as 'the defeated one'. The use of one of the ships from the Greek fleet, in fact, could have been read as the sign of the surrendering of one of the princes listed in Homer's 'catalogue of ships', and not as a full Trojan victory. As stated above, also in this case, nothing should have sound strange to the Trojans. An Ugaritic text reports in fact the use of a single ship to bring tributes from several different bearers to one king

> Hundred ten/twenty...copper is lost in a ship
> 20 for the people from Umd
> 10 for Kutilana.[62]

Homeric narrations inform us that the ἵππος ship was not borrowed, it was built by the Achaeans under Athena Pallas' guidance. With regard to this specific circumstance, the involvement of Epeius is also a key element for the correct flowing of the plan. Epeius was not a shipwright, nor a craftsman, therefore he could follow the goddess' instructions without the risk of building a suspect Greek-shape ship. On the other hand, Pallas was not only the Achaeans protector, she was also the deity to whom was dedicated the Trojan temple on the top of the citadel, she would have been extremely familiar with the Levantine technical and shipbuilding traditions.

Thus, read in its naval dimension, the deception of the so-called Wooden Horse of Troy planned by Athena resulted in a successful plan. As reported by Lydos

> περὶ τοῦ δουρεου ἵππου ό Εὐφοριων φησὶ πλοῖον γενέσται τοῖς ῞Ελλησιν ἵππον λεγόμενων,
>
> concerning the wooden horse, Euphorion says it was a boat called Horse by the Greeks[63]

and we can say, with Cecil Torr, that Euphorion of Chalchis[64] was completely right when noting that 'in the legend of the taking of Troy through the stratagem conceived by Athena, there is a reminiscence of the capture of some seaport town by men concealed on board a ship, which had unwarily been admitted within the harbour'.[65]

More precisely, we can say that, speaking of the last night of Troy, Homer spoke of the 'merchant ship' (πλοῖον) 'made of planks' (δουρατεον) 'named horse' (ἵππον λεγόμενων) used to break the siege. This was the homeric *ἵππος* of Troy.

---

[61] Lipinksi 1971: 87.
[62] Text: KTU 4.394
[63] Lydos, *De Mensibus* IV.88.
[64] Greek poet and grammarian, born at Chalcis in Euboea about 275 BC, who was invited about 221 to the court of Syria by Antiochus the Great and assisted in the formation of the royal Library of Antioch, of which he held the post of librarian till his death. He wrote mythological epics (Thrax), elegies, epigrams, and satirical poems (Fragments by Euphorion are published in Meinke A., 1843, *De Euphorionis Chalcidensis vita e scriptis*. Analecta Alexandrina).
[65] Euphorion of Calchis, *fragment* 120; Torr 1896: 114.

From the ship to the wooden horse of Troy

Despite Homer never spoke of a colossal wooden simulacre in shape of a horse, as discussed above, the passage from history to legend, which appears to have been extremely rapid, transformed the iconography of the episode definitely.

From at least the seventh-sixth centuries BC onward, most of the images referring of Athena's deception became rather mythological or sacral depictions rather than historic representations. The dedication of horses to Artemis and Athena might be the milestone for this change.[66]

The parallel between the evolution of the iconography and of the narration appears to be more evident during the Roman era, particularly from the second half of the first century BC onward. In fact, while on the one hand the new version of the last night of Troy, as presented in the second book of the Vergil's Aeneid, finally fixed the still-nowadays-shared account of the events for the whole successive iconography of the Trojan Horse, on the other hand the effect of the diffusion of the Vergil's narration, even in its iconographic versions, seems to have affected also some of the later known versions of the Last Night of Troy.

Vergil's work also continued to influence later written accounts and iconography as well, and the idea of the giant wooden quadruped, implausible to Homer's audience, became widely accepted and was fixed, for modern-days audience, by modern-days translations, paintings, and movies. Diffused and strongly rooted in modern culture, the idea of the horse has recently entered also the IT world.

This is not the sole case of a misunderstanding that has become a certain truth. Just to have an idea of how and why this happens, we can draw a parallel between the episode of the *hippos ship* of Troy in the Sacred Books of the early Greeks, and that of the Red Sea Crossing narrated in the Holy Bible.

According to what reported in the book of the Exodus of St Jerome's *Vulgata*, dated about 400 CE:

> [19]tollensque se angelus Dei qui praecedebat castra Israhel abiit post eos et cum eo
> pariter columna nubis priora dimittens post tergum[20] stetit inter castra Aegyptiorum
> et castttra Israhel et erat nubes tenebrosa et inluminans noctem ut ad se invicem toto
> noctis temport accedere non valerent[21] cumque extendisset Moses manum super mare
> abstulit illud Dominus flante vento vehementi et urente tota nocte et vertit in siccum
> divisaque est aqua[22] et ingressi sunt filii Israhel per medium maris sicci erat enim aqua
> quasi murus a dextra eorum et leva[23] persequentesque Aegyptii ingress sunt post eos
> ominis equitatus currus eius et equites per medium maris[24] iamque advenerat vigilia
> matutina et ecce respiciens Dominus super castra Aegyptiorum per columnam ignis
> et nubis interfecit eorum[25] et subeverit rotas curruum ferebanurque in profundum
> dixerunt ergo Aegyptii fugiamus Israhelem Dominus enim pugnat pro eis contra nos.[19]

[66] Nadal 2005, D'Agostino 2007.

> The angel of God, who went before the camp of Israel, moved and went behind them; and the pillar of cloud moved from before them, and stood behind them.[20] It came between the camp of the Egyptians and the camp of Israel; and there was the cloud and the darkness, yet gave it light by night: and the one didn't come near the other all the night.[21] Moses stretched out his hand over the sea, and Yahweh caused the sea to go back by a strong east wind all the night, and made the sea dry land, and the waters were staved off [22] and the children of Israel went into the midst of the dry sea, and the waters were similar to a wall to them on their right hand, and on their left.[23] The Egyptians pursued, and went in after them into the midst of the sea: all of Pharaoh's horses, his chariots, and his horsemen.[24] It happened in the morning watch, that Yahweh looked out on the host of the Egyptians through the pillar of fire and of cloud, and confused the Egyptian army.[25] He took off their chariot wheels, and they drove them heavily; so that Egyptians said, "Let's flee from the face of Israel, for Yahwe fights for them against the Egyptians!"[67]

The medieval iconography of this episode, as shown in the Sistina Chapel at Rome, used to depict the children of Israel safe on the shore, on the other side of the Red Sea, while the chariots and the soldiers of the Egyptian army are shown bogged down in a sort of swamp, pointing back to Pharaoh's reign.

However, contemporary interpretation of this episode appears to be strongly influenced by Hollywood filmography, widespread and commonly accepted by the majority of the modern-days people. This new version of the Red Sea Crossing sees 'Moses-Charlton Eston' standing on the top of a rock, with a Pastoral in his right end, commanding the Sea to open. The waters retire and create a sort of highway in the middle of the Sea, permitting the children of Israel to pass safe. Then, the two massive water-walls fall down from the two sides of the passage, drowning and killing the Egyptian army that had almost reached the fugitives.

Apparently marginal, this distortion of what reported in the Bible has determined the choice by some modern-days researchers to arrange pseudo-scientific expeditions and operations in the northern part of the Red Sea in search for the 'drowned Pharaoh's armada'. Like it happened for the Trojan *hippos*, later versions of the episode have determined a radical change in the interpretation of a crucial episode of the religious history of a side of the World.

[67] The Holy Bible, *Exodus* XIV.19-25.

Bibliography

AA.VV., 1655, *Lexicon Philologicum Praecipue Etymologicum et Sacrum in quo Latinae et a Latinibus Autoris.*

Ackermann, H.C. and J.-R. Gisler (eds.). 1981-99. *Lexicon Iconographicum Mythologiae Classicae*, 16 pts in 8 vols and indexes (Zurich: Artemis).

Albenda, P. 1983. 'A Mediterranean Seascape from Khorsabad. Assur', *Undena*, 3.3: 1-34.

Albenda, P. 1986. *The palace of Sargon, king of Assyria: monumental wall reliefs at Dur-Sharrukin, from original drawings made at the time of their discovery in 1843-1844 by Botta and Flandin* (Paris: Éds. Recherche sur les Civilisations).

Almagro Gorbea, M. 1977. El Bronce Final y el período orientalizante en Extremadura, *Biblioteca Praehistorica Hispana*, XIV (Madrid)

Anderson, J. K. 1961. *Ancient Greek Hosemanship* (Berkeley and Los Angeles).

Anderson, M. J. 1997. *The Fall of Troy in Early Greek Poetry and Art.* (Oxford: Oxford University Press).

Austin, R. G. 1959. 'Virgil and the Wooden Horse', *The Journal of Roman Studies*, 49.1-2: 16-25.

Austin, R. G. 1964. *Aeneidos: Liber secundus.* (Oxford: Clarendon Press).

Austin, R. G. 1980. *Aeneid, Liber 2* (Oxford: Clarendon Press).

Avigad, N. 1966. 'A Hebrew Seal with a Family Emblem', *Israel Exploration Journal*, 16: 50-53.

Avigad, N. 1981. 'On Titles and Symbols on Hebrew Seals', *Eretz- Israel*, 15: 303-05.

Avigad, N. 1982. 'A Hebrew Seal Depicting a Sailing Ship', *Bulletin of the American Schools of Oriental Research*, 246: 59-62.

Baldacci, M. 2017. *Le origini della navigazione. Mesopotamia e Mediterraneo antico.* (Lecce: Capone Editore).

Barchiesi, A. 1984. *La traccia del modello, effetti omerici nella narrazione virgiliana* (Pisa: Giardini).

Barnett, R.D. 1958. 'Early Shipping in the Near East', *Antiquity*, XXXII: 220-234

Basch, L. 1969. 'Phoenician Oared Ships', *The Mariners' Mirror*, 55.1: 139-162.

Basch, L. 1987. *Le Musée Imaginaire de la Marine Antique.* (Athens: Institute Hellénique pour la préservation des traditions Nautiques).

Basch, L. 1988. 'The Eleusis Museum Trireme and the Athenian Trireme', *Mariner's Mirror*, 74.2: 163-188.

Bass, G.F. 1961. 'The Cape Gelidonya wreck: preliminary report', *American Journal of Archaeology*, 65.3, pp. 267-276

Bass, G.F. 1967. 'Cape Gelidonya: a Bronze Age shipwreck', *Transactions of the American Philosophical Society*, 57.8

Bass, G.F. 1972. 'The earliest seafarers in the Mediterranean and the Near East', in G. F. Bass (ed.), *A history of Seafaring based on Underwater Archaeology* (London: Thames and Hudson), pp. 11-36.

Bass, G.F. 1986. 'A Bronze Age Shipwreck at Ulu Burun (Kaş): 1984 Campaign', *American Journal of Archaeology*: 269-296.

Bass, G.F. 1999, The Hull and Anchor of the Cape Gelidonya Ship, in Ph. Betancourt, V. Karageorghis, R. Laffineur, W.D. Niemeier (eds.), *Meletemata. Studies in Aegean Archaeology presented to Malcom H. Wiener*, *Aegaeum*, 20, Liège, pp. 21-24

Bass, G. F., et al. 1989. 'The Bronze Age Shipwreck at Ulu Burun: 1986 Campaign', *American Journal of Archaeology*: 1-29.

Beckman, G., 1995. 'Royal ideology and State Administration in Hittite Anatolia', in J.M. Sasson (ed) *Civilization of the Ancient Near East*, I (New York: Charles Scribner's sons), pp. 529-43.

Beckman, G., Bryce T., Cline, E.H. 2011. *The Ahhiyawa Texts* (Atlanta: The Society of Biblical Literature).

Benini, A. 2012. 'Lo scafo. Madieri, schedatura preliminare', in D. Vullo (ed.), *La nave Greca arcaica di Gela, dallo scavo al recupero*, (Palermo: Regione Siciliana), pp. 53-105.

Bernardini, P. 2014. *I Fenici tra il vicino Oriente e la Sardegna.* (Sassari: Carlo Delfino).

Beschi, F., 2013. *La Leggenda di Troia* (Torino: Einaudi).

Bielman Sanchez, A. 2007. 'La guerre de Troie ou la défaite des femmes ?', in D. Van Mal-Maeder (ed) *Le cheval de Troie. Variations autour d'une guerre* (Gollion: Infolio), pp. 59-99.

Blackman, D.J. 1982a. 'Ancient Harbours in the Mediterranean', *International journal of Nautical Archaeology*, 11.2: 79-104.

Blackman, D.J. 1982b. 'Ancient Harbours in the Mediterranean', *International journal of Nautical Archaeology*, 11.3: 185-221.

Blackman, D.J. *1990.* 'Triremes and *shipsheds'*, in H. Tzalas (Ed.), *Tropis II. 2nd International Symposium on Ship Construction in Antiquity, Delphi 1987*, pp. 35-52.

Blackman, D.J. 2014. 'Research and Investigation of Ancient Shipsheds' in D. Blackman (ed.), *Shipsheds of the Ancient Mediterranean* (Cambridge: Cambridge University Press).

Blegen C.W., 1963, *Troy and the Trojans*, Praeger, New York, 145.

Blegen C.W., Caskey J.L., Rawson M., 1953, *Troy III: The Sixth Settlement*, Princeton University Press, Princeton, p. 331.

Blegen C.W., Caskey J.L., Rawson M., 1958 *Troy IV: Settlements VIIa,VIIb and VIII*, Princeton University Press, Princeton, 11-12.

Boardman, J. 1991. The sixth-century potters and painters of Athens and their public, *Looking at Greek vases, 82.*

Boardman, J. 1994. *Greek Arts* (London: Thames and Hudson).

Boardman, J. 2014. 'Homer and the Legacy of the Age of Heroes', in J. Aruz, S. B. Graff, and Y. Rakic (eds), *Assyria to Iberia at the Dawn of the Classical Age*, (New York: The Metropolitan Museum of Art), pp. 24-32.

Boetto, G., Koncani Uhac, I., Uhac, M., 2014. 'Navires de l'âge du Bronze à l'époque romaine enIstrie', *Dossier d'Archéologie - Ports et navires dans l'antiquité et à l'époque byzantine*, 364, pp. 22-25

Bondì, S. F. 1988. 'Le Origini in Oriente', in S. Moscati (ed.), *I Fenici* (Milano: Bompiani), pp. 28-37.

Botta, E.1849. *Monuments de Ninive* (Paris : Imprimerie Nationale).

Calonghi, F. 1950, *Dizionario Latino-Italiano* (Torino: Rosenberg & Seller).

Cancik-Kirschbaum, E. 2003. *Gli Assiri* (Bologna: Il Mulino)

Casson, L. 1970. 'Another Note on Phoenician Galleys', *The Mariners' Mirror*, 56.4: 340.

Casson, L. 1971. *Ships and Seamanship in the Ancient World.* (Princeton: Princeton University Press).

Casson, L. 1994. *Ships and Seafaring in ancient times.* (Austin: Texas University press).

Casson, L. 2007. 'Homeric Seafaring-by Samuel Mark', *International Journal of Nautical Archaeology* 36.1: 197-199.

Celestino S. Blanco J.L., 2006, 'La joyería en los orígenes de Extremadura: el espejo de los dioses', *Estudios históricos de Lusitania*, 1

Celestino Pérez S., Salgado Carmona J. Á., 2007, *Fenicios e indígenas a través del tesoro de Aliseda*, Barcelona

Clausen, W. 2002. 'Virgil's Aeneid', *Decorum, Allusion, and Ideology* (Munich: Saur).
Claverhouse J.R., Headlam W.G., Pearson A.C. (eds). 1917. *The fragments of Sophocles.* Vol. 1. (Cambridge: Cambirdge University Press).
Cline, E. H. 2014. *1177 avant J-C. Le jour où la civilisation s'est effondrée.* (Paris: La Découverte)
Cline, E. H. 2018. *La Guerra di Troia* (Milano: Hoepli).
Cline E.H., Yasur-Landau A. 2007. 'Musings from a Distant Shore: The Nature and Destination of the Uluburun Ship and its Cargo', *Tel Aviv*, 34:2: 125-141.
Cline E.H., O'Connor D. 2012, 'The Sea Peoples', in Cline, O'Connor (eds.), *Ramesses III: the Life and Times od Egypt's last Hero*, (Ann Arbor:University of Michigan Press).
Conington, J. 1876. *P. Vergili Maronis Opera.* Vol. 2. (London: Whittaker and Company).
Cultraro, M. 2006. *I Micenei* (Roma: Carocci).
Curtis J., Tallis N. (eds.), 2008. *The Balawat Gates of Ashurnasirpal II* (London: British Museum Publications Limited).
Curtis J., Tallis N. (eds.), 2012. 'The horse in the Ancient Near East', in J. Curtis, N. Tallis (eds) *The Horse from Arabia to Royal Ascott* (London: British Museum Publications Limited), pp. 14-27.
D'agostino, B. 1967. 'Osservazioni a proposito della guerra lelantina', *Dialoghi di Archeologia*, I: 20-37.
D'agostino, B. 2007. 'The Trojan Horse: Between Athena and Artemis', *Annali di Archeologia e Storia Antica*, n.s., 13-14: 185-196.
Davies, M. 1989. 'The Date of the Epic Cycle', *Glotta* 67.1./2. H: 89-100.
Davies, N. 1963. *Scenes from some Theban Tombs, Private Tombs at Thebes*, IV (Oxford University Press)
Davies, N. De G., Faulkner, O. 1947. 'A Syrian Trading Venture to Egypt', *The Journal of Egyptian Archaeology*, 33: 40-46.
De Graeve, M.C. 1981. *The ships of the Ancient Near East (2000 – 500 BC)* (Leven: Departement Oriëntalistiek).
De Juan, C. 2014. 'Les épaves de Mazarròn et de Binissafùller. La tradition ibérique d'influence punico-phénicienne', *Dossier d'Archéologie - Ports et navires dans l'antiquité et à l'époque byzantine*, 364, pp. 25-33.
Dell'Amico, P. 2008. 'Rivisitazione del relitto di Golo ed alcune considerazioni in merito', *Archaeologia Maritima Mediterranea*, 5, pp. 13-22
Dickinson, O. 2006. *The Aegean from Bronze Age to Iron Age* (London: Routledge).
Dörpfeld W., 1902, *Troja und Ilion: Ergebnisse der Ausgrabungen in den vorhistorischen und hisorischen Schichten von Ilion, 1870-1894*, (Athens: Beck & Narth).
Drews, R., 2010. *Guerrieri a Cavallo. I primi cavalieri in Asia Centrale e in Europa (4000-900 a.C.)* (Gorizia: LGM).
Elat, M. 1977. *Economic relations in the lands of the Bible: c. 1000-539 BC* (Haifa: The Bialik Institute).
Elayi, J. 2017. *Sargon II, King of Assyria* (Atlanta: SBL Press).
Elayi, J., Elayi, A. G. 2005. 'Ba'al Arwad', in A. Spanò Giammellaro (ed) *Atti del V Congresso Internazionale di Studi Fenicio-Punici, Marsala 2000*, pp. 101-2.
Ervin, M. 1964. 'A relief pithos from Mykonos', *Archaeologicon Delton*, 18: 37-75.
Ervin-Caskey, M. 1976. 'Notes on the relief-pithoi of the Tenian-Boeotioan group', *American Journal of Archaeology*, 80.1: 19-41.
Escacena Carrasco J.L., Fernández Flores Á., Rodríguez Azogue A. 2007. 'Sobre el Carambolo: un híppos sagrado del santuario IV y su contexto arqueológico', *Archivo español de arqueología*, 80: 5-28.

Etienne, R. 2005. 'Hippotrophia, aspects sociaux de l'élevage des chevaux en Grèce', in A. Gardeisen (ed) *Les Équidés Dans Le Monde Méditerranéen Antique: Actes Du Colloque Organisé Par L'Ecole Française D'Athènes, Le Centre Camille Jullian Et L'UMR 5140 Du CNRS, Athènes, 26-28 Novembre 2003*. (Rousillon: Éd. de l'Association pour le développement de l'archéologie en Languedoc), pp. 243-8.

Fantar, M. H. 2004. 'I Fenici', in M. Guidetti (ed) *Storia del Mediterraneo nell'antichità* (Milano: Jaca Book), pp. 15-45

Fantuzzi, M., Tsagalis, C. 2015. *The Greek Epic Cycle and its Ancient Reception: a Companion*. (Cambridge University Press).

Finley, M. 2002. *The World of Odysseus* (New York: Review Books)

Fiorentini, G. 1994. 'Attività di indagini archeologiche della Soprintendenza Beni Culturali e Ambientali di Agrigento. Area sacra di Via Venezia', *Kokalos* 39-40:.722-723.

Fitton, L. J., Villing A. 2019. 'Storytellers', in A. Villing, J.L. Fitton, V. Donnellan, A. Shapland (eds), *Troy. Myth and Reality* (London: Thames and Hudson), pp. 16-50.

Fitzgerald, A. 1997. 'Uluburun', *British Museum Encyclopaedia of Underwater and Maritime Archaeology, London*, pp. 430-432.

Fontan, E. 2014. 'Fragments of band with Phoenician Tribute Bearers', in J. Aruz, S. B. Graff, and Y. Rakic (eds), *Assyria to Iberia at the Dawn of the Classical Age* (New York: The Metropolitan Museum of Art), pp. 136-7.

Franko, G.F. 2006. 'The Trojan Horse at the Close of the Iliad', *The Classical Journal*. 101.2: 121-123

Friedman, Z., 2015. 'The Phoenician *Hippos* Figurehead. Preserved Tradition and Types of Ship', in R. K. Pedersen (ed.), *On Sea and Ocean: New Research in Phoenician Seafaring Proceedings of the Symposion held in Marburg, June 23–25, 2011at Archäologisches Seminar, Philipps-Universität Marburg*, pp. 19-34.

Frost, H. 1981. 'Lilybaeum (Marsala)—The Punic Ship: Final Excavation Report', *Notizie dagli Scavi di Antichità*, Serie 8, Supplemento 30.

Frost, H, Werner A.E., Oddy W.A., 1973. 'First season of excavation on the Punic wreck in Sicily', *International Journal of Nautical Archaeology*, 2.1: 33-49.

Fuchs, M. 2007, 'Comme sur des roulettes. Le cheval de Troie vision Romaine', in D. Van Mal-Maeder (ed), *Le cheval de Troie. Variations autour d'une guerre* (Gollion : Infolio), pp. 13-31.

Ghali-Kahil, L.B. 1955. *Les enlèvements et le retour d'Hélène dans les textes et les documents figurés* (Paris: De Boccard).

Graff, B. 2014. 'Kingdom of Midas and Croesus', in J. Aruz, S. B. Graff, and Y. Rakic (eds), *Assyria to Iberia at the Dawn of the Classical Age*, (New York: The Metropolitan Museum of Art), pp. 104-109.

Gras, M. 1992. 'La mémoire de Lixus. De la fondation de Lixus aux premiers rapports entre Grecs et Phéniciens an Afrique du Nord', *Lixus. Atti del colloquio di Larache 1989*, (Roma: Ecole Française de Rome), pp. 27-44.

Gras, M. 2000. 'La battaglia del Mare Sardonio', in P. Bernardini, P.G. Spanu, R. Zucca (eds), *Màxe. La Battaglia del Mare Sardonio. Studi e Ricerche*, (Oristano-Cagliari: La Memoria Storica-Mythos), pp. 37-46.

Gray, D. 1974. *Seewesen*. Archeologia Homerica, Vol. 1 (Ruprecht Gmbh & Co.)

Grayson, A. K., 1991. 'Assyrian Rulers of the Early First Millennium BC I (1114-895)', *The Royal inscription of the Mesopotamia – Assirian period. Vol. 2* (Toronto University Press)

Grayson, A. K., 1996. 'Assyrian Rulers of the Early First Millennium BC II (858-745 BC)', *The Royal inscription of the Mesopotamia – Assirian period. Vol. 3* (Toronto University Press)

Griffin, J. 1977, 'The epic cycle and the uniqueness of Homer', *The journal of Hellenic studies*, 97: 39-53.
Grimal, P. 1990. *Enciclopedia della Mitologia* (Milano: Garzanti).
Grote, G. 1856. *History of Greece* (New York: Harper & Brothers)
Guerrero Ayuso, V.M., Escacena Carrasco J. 2010. 'Barca ritual fenicia en el santuario de "El Carambolo"', in S. Meads, M. D'Agostino, G. Caniato (eds), *Atti del I Convegno Nazionale di Archeologia, Storia ed Etnologia Navale*, NAVIS, 4, pp. 239-250
Guibal, F., Pomey, P. 2003. 'Timber supply and ancient naval architecture', in C. Beltrame (ed) *Boats, Ships and Shipyards: Proceedings of the Ninth International Symposium on Boat and Ship Archaeology, Venice 2000* (London: Oxbow Books Limited), pp. 35-41.
Guzzo, P. L. 2011. Fondazioni Greche (Roma: Carocci Editore)
Hampe R., 1936. *Frühe griechische Sagenbinder in Böotien.* (Athens: Deutsches Archäologische. Institut)
Harvard 1938. The Phoenician Merchantman. *Bulletin of the Business Historical Society*, 12.4: 58-60.
Hawkins, J.D. 1998. 'Tarkasnawa King of Mira 'Tarkondemos' Boğazköy Sealing and Karabel, *Anatolian Studies*, 48: 1-31.
Hedreen, G. 1996. 'Image, text, and story in the recovery of Helen', *Classical Antiquity* 15.1, pp. 152-184.
Hertel, D. 2001. *Troia* (Bologna: Il Mulino).
Hoftijzer J., Van Soldt W.H. 1998. Texts from Ugarit Pertaining to Seafaring, in S. Wachsmann, *Seagoing ships seamanship of the Bronze Age Levant* (College Station: Texas A&M University Press), pp. 333-44.
Ieranò, G. 2015. Gli eroi della guerra di Troia. (Venezia: Sonzogno).
Ingoglia, C. 2000. 'Il cavallo di Troia su una" Kotyle" corinzia da Gela e nell'Ilioupersis di Arctino', *Quaderni Urbinati di Cultura Classica*, 65.2, pp. 7-14.
Jacoby, R. 1991. 'The representation and identification of cities on Assyrian reliefs', *Israel Exploration Journal*: 112-131.
Janni, P. 1996. *Il Mare degli antichi* (Bari: Dedalo).
Johansen F., 1967. *The Iliad in Early Greek Art* (Copenhagen: Munkksgaard).
Johnstone, P. 1973. 'Stern first in the Stone Age?', *The International Journal of Nautical Archaeology*, 2.1: 3-11.
Johnstone, P. 1989. *The Sea-craft of prehistory* (London: Thames and Hudson)
Jones, J. W. 1970. 'The Trojan horse: timeo Danaos et dona ferentis', *The Classical Journal*, *65*(6): 241-247.
Kahanov, Y., Pomey, P. 2004. 'The Greek Sewn Shipbuilding Tradition and the Ma'agan Mikhael Ship: A Comparison with Mediterranean Parallels from the Sixth to the Fourth Centuries BC', *The Mariner's Mirror*, 90.1: 6-28.
King, L.W. 1915. *Bronze Reliefs from the Gates of Shalmaneser, King of Assyria B.C. 860–825*, (London: Print by order of the Trustees).
Knauer, G. N. 1964.,'Vergil's *Aeneid* and Homer', *Greek, Roman and Byzantine Studies*, 5.2: 50-65.
Korfmann M., 2004, 'Die Arbeiten in Troia/Wilusa 2003; Work at Troia/Wilusa in 2003', *Studia Troica, 14.*
Korou, N. 2002. 'Phéniciens, Chypriotes, Eubéens et la fondation de Carthage', *Centre d'Etude Chypriote, Cahiers*, 32: 89-114.
Kurt, C. 1979. *Seemänische Fachausdrücke bei Homer. Unter berücksichtigung Hesiods und der Lyriker bis Bakchylides.* (Göttingen:Vandenhoeck & Ruprecht)

Latacz, J. 2004. *Troy and Homer: Towards a Solution of an Old Mystery*, Oxford.
Layard, A. H. 1849a. *The Monuments of Nineveh: from drawings made on the spot, during a second expedition to Assyria: 1st series* (Murray).
Layard, A. H. 1849b. *The Monuments of Nineveh: from drawings made on the spot, during a second expedition to Assyria: 2nd series* (Murray).
Lenormant, F. 1878. 'Bas-reliefs de Bronze Assyriens', *Gazette Archéologique*, IV : 119-129.
Linder, E. 1986. 'The Khorsabad Wall Relief: A Mediterranean Seascape or River Transport of Timbers?', *Journal of the American Oriental Society*, 106: 273-81.
Lipinski, E. 1971. 'Epiphanie de Baal-Haddu - RS 24.245', *Ugarit-Forschungen*, 3: 88.
Lippolis, E., Rocco, G. 2011. *Archeologia Greca. Cultura, società, politica e produzione* (Milano: Mondadori).
Liverani, M. 2017. *Assiria*. (Roma-Bari:Laterza).
Lowenstam, S. 1974. 'Talking vases: the relationship between the Homeric poems and archaic representations of epic myth', *Transactions of the American Philological Association*,127: 21-76.
Loyd, A. B. 1975. 'Were Necho's Triremes Phoenician?', *The Journal of Hellenic Studies*, 95: 45-61.
Luzon, J.M.. 1988. 'Los Hippoi Gaditanos', in *I Congreso Internacional sobre el Estrecho de Gibraltar, Ceuta 1987*, Vol. 1, pp. 445-458.
Maiuri, A. 1933. *La Casa del Menandro e il suo tesoro di argenteria*. Roma
Marangou C., 2003. 'Neolithic Watercraft in Greece: Circumstantial evidence and Serious Guesses', in C. Beltrame (ed), *Boats, Ships and Shipyards, Proceedings of the 9th ISBSA Venice*, (London: Oxbow), pp. 14-18
Mark, S. E. 1991. 'Odyssey 5.234-53 and Homeric ship construction: a reappraisal, *American Journal of Archaeology*, 95.3: 441-445.
Mark, S. E. 2005. *Homeric seafaring*. (College Station: Texas A&M University Press).
Markoe, G. 1996. 'The emergence of orientalizing in Greek art: Some observations on the interchange between Greeks and Phoenicians in the eighth and seventh centuries BC', *Bulletin of the American Schools of Oriental Research*, 301: 47-67.
McGrail, S. 1985, 'Towards a classification of water transports', *World Archaeology*, 16.3: 289-303.
McGrail, S. 2000. *Boats of the World*. (Oxford: Oxford University Press).
Medas, S. 2000. *La Marineria Cartaginese* (Sassari: Carlo Delfino)
Meineke, A. 1843. *Analecta Alexandrina* (Berlin).
Miguélez-Cavero, L. 2013. *Triphiodorus," The sack of Troy": a general study and a commentary*, (Berlin: de Gruyter).
Minano A., 2014, 'El Barco 2 de Mazarròn'. *ARQUA*, pp. 1-15.
Morrison, J. S., Williams, R. T. 1968. *Greek Oared Ships 900-322 B.C.*, (Cambridge: Cambridge University Press).
Moscati, S. 1988. 'La colonizzazione Mediterranea', in S. Moscati (ed.), *I Fenici* (Milano: Bompiani), pp. 46-53
Mountjoy P.A. 1991, 'The Destruction of Troy VIh', *Studia Troica*, 9, pp. 253-93
Mountjoy P.A. 1999b, 'Troy VII reconsidered', *Studia Troica*, 9, pp. 295-346
Müller, M. W. 1904. *Neue Darstellungen ‚mykenischer' Gesandter und phónizischer Schiffe in altagyptischen Wandgemälden: Mit 5 tafeln und vielen textabbildungen.* (Peiser)
Muscarella, O. 1998. 'Relations between Phrygia and Assyria in the eighth century BC', *XXIV Uluslararası Assiriyoloji Kongresi*, pp. 149-157.
Nadal, E. 2005. 'Poséidon Hippios, les cheveaux et les cavaliers à travers la céramique', in A. Gardeisen (ed) *Les Équidés Dans Le Monde Méditerranéen Antique: Actes Du Colloque Organisé*

Par L'Ecole Française D'Athènes, Le Centre Camille Jullian Et L'UMR 5140 Du CNRS, Athènes, 26-28 Novembre 2003. (Rousillon: Éd. de l'Association pour le développement de l'archéologie en Languedoc), pp. 111-136.

Negueruela, I. 2005. '"Cogamenta punicana" e bagli. La costruzione navale a fasciame portante tra i fenici del VII secolo a.C', in B.M Giannattasio, C. Canepa, L. Grasso, E. Piccardi (eds), *Aequora, pontos, Jam, mare... Mare, uomini e merci nel Mediterraneo antico, Atti del convegno di Genova,* (Borgo San Lorenzo: All'insegna del Giglio), pp. 22-41.

Negueruela, I., Ortiz, P. 2004. 'Hacia la comprensión de la construcción naval fenicia según el barco «Mazarrón-2» del siglo VII a.C.', *La Navegación Fenicia: Tecnología Naval y Derroteros, Centro de Estudios Fenicios y Púnicos,* Madrid, pp. 227-278.

Negueruela, I., Pinedo, J., Gömez, M., Miñano, A., Arellano, I., Barba, J.S. 1995. 'Seventh-century BC Phoenician vessel discovered at Playa de la Isla, Mazarron, Spain', *The International Journal of Nautical Archaeology*, 24.3, pp. 189-197.

Negueruela, I., Miñano, A., Frutos, J.B., Pinedo, J., Gómez, M., Arellano, I. 2000. 'Descubrimiento de dos barcos fenicios en Mazarrón (Murcia)', *Actas del IV Congreso Internacional de Estudios Fenicios y Púnicos: Cádiz, 2 al 6 de octubre de 1995*, pp. 1671-1679.

Negueruela, I., Gallero, R.G., Claudio, M.S., Sanmartín, A.M., Presa, M., Marín, C. 2004. 'Mazarrón-2: el barco fenicio del siglo VII aC Campaña de noviembre-1999/marzo 2000', *El mundo púnico. Religión, antropología y cultura material. Actas II Congreso Internacional del Mundo Púnico*, Cartagena, pp. 453-483.

Nicolini, G. 1991. *Techniques des ors antiques. La bijouterie ibérique du VIIe au IV siècle* (Condésur-Noireau).

Nougayrol, Jean, 1960. 'Nouveaux textes accadiens de Ras-Shamra', *Comptes rendus des séances de l'Académie des Inscriptions et Belles-Lettres*, 104. 1: 163-171.

Nucci, F., Orsini, S. 2003. 'Informations nouvelles sur l'épave antique retrouvée près de Mariana', *Cahiers Corsica*, 209-210: 1-40

Paris F.E., 1892, *Souvenirs de marine conservés, 5e partie*, (Paris : Imp. Nat.)

Peyronnel, L. 2008. *Storia e Archeologia del Commercio nell'Oriente Antico* (Roma: Carocci).

Polzer, M. 2010. 'The VIth-Century BC Shipwreck at Pabuç Burnu, Turkey. Evidence for Transition from Lacing to Mortise-and-Tenon Joinery in Late Archaic Greek Shipbuilding', in P. Pomey (ed) *Transferts technologiques en architecture navale méditerranéenne de l'Antiquité aux temps modernes: identité technique et identité culturelle, Actes de la Table Ronde Internationale d'Istanbul, 19-21 mai 2007,Varia Anatolica* XXX : 27–44

Polzer, M. 2014. 'The Bajo de la Campana Shipwreck and Colonial Trade in Phoenician Spain', in J. Aruz, S. B. Graff, and Y. Rakic (eds), *Assyria to Iberia at the Dawn of the Classical Age*, (New York: The Metropolitan Museum of Art), pp. 230-242.

Pomey, P. 1996. 'Navigazione e navi all'epoca della colonizzazione', in G. Pugliese Carratelli (ed), *I Greci in occidente* (Milano: Bompiani), pp. 133-140.

Pomey, P. 1997. *La Navigation dans l'Antiquité* (Aix-en-Provence: Edisud).

Pomey, P. 2009. 'Des bateaux cousus aux bateaux à tenons et mortaises. Un exemple d'évolution des techniques de construction navale', in X. Nieto, M. Cau (eds), *Arqueologia Nàutica Mediterrània, Monografie del CASC*, 8: 357-364.

Pomey, P. 2012. 'Le dossier de l'épave du Golo (Mariana, Haute-Corde)', *Archeonautica*, 17: 11-30.

Pomey, P., Poveda, P. 2015. *Le Gyptis. Reconstruction d'un navire antique* (Paris : CNRS Edition)

Pomey, P., Rieth, E. 2005. *L'Archéologie Navale*, (Paris: Errance).

Pomey, P., Kahanov Y., Rieth E. 2012. 'Transition from Shell to Skeleton in Ancient Mediterranean Ship-Construction: analysis, problems, and future research', *International Journal of Nautical Archaeology*, 41.2: 235-314.

Pulak, C. 1988. 'The Bronze Age Shipwreck at Ulu Burun, Turkey: 1985 Campaign', *American Journal of Archaeology*: 1-37.

Pulak, C. 1997. 'The Uluburun Shipwreck', in: S. Swiny, R.L. der Hohlfel, H.. W. Swiny (eds.), *Res Maritime: Cyprus and the Eastern Mediterranean from Prehistory to Late Antiquity* (Atlanta, GA), pp. 233-262

Pulak, C. 2003, Mortise-and-Tenon Joints of Bronze Age Seagoing Ships, in C. Beltrame (ed), *Boats, Ships and Shipyards, Proceedings of the 9th ISBSA Venice*, London, pp. 28-34

Rand, H., 2015. 'What was the Trojan Horse?', *Vulcan*, *3*(1): 1-18.

Rapp G., 1982, 'Earthquakes in the Troad', in Rapp G. Gifforf G.A. (eds.) *Troy: The Archaeological Geology*, (Princeton: Princeton University Press), pp.43-58.

Reade, J. 1976. 'Sargon's Campaigns of 720, 716, and 715 BC: Evidence from the Sculptures', *Journal of Near Eastern Studies*, 35.2: 95-104

Reade, J. 1979. 'Ideology and propaganda in Assyrian art', in *Power and propaganda: A symposium on ancient empires*, Vol. 7 (Copenhagen), pp. 329-343.

Reber, K. 2007. 'Troie, Découverte et état actuel', in D. Van Mal-Maeder (ed) *Le cheval de Troie. Variations autour d'une guerre* (Gollion: Infolio), pp. 13-31.

Ribichini, S. 2000. 'Sui miti della fondazione di Cadice' in *Actas del IV Congreso Internacional de Estudios Fenicios y Púnicos*, Vol. 2 (Cádiz 1995), pp. 661-668.

Ringel, J.1984. *Maritime Motifs on Ancient Coins at the National Maritime Museum Haifa* (Haifa: American Friends of the National Maritime Museum).

Rival, M. 1991. '*La charpenterie navale romaine: matériaux, méthodes, moyens*' (Paris : Editions du CNRS).

Rossi, L. E. 1977. 'I poemi omerici come testimonianza di poesia orale', in R. Bianchi Bandinelli (ed) *Storia e civiltà dei Greci*, I (Milano: Bompiani), pp. 73-147.

Rubino, M., 2012. Note al libro secondo, in C. Vivaldi (ed.), *Virgilio. Eneide*, pp. 408-413.

Ruiz de Arbulo Bayona, Joaquín. 2009. 'Los navegantes y lo sagrado. El barco de Troya. Nuevos argumentos para una explicación náutica del caballo de madera' *Arqueologia nàutica mediterrània Monografie del CASC*, 8: 535-550.

Sadurska, A. 1986. 'Equus Troianus', *Lexicon Iconographicum Mithologiaae Classicae*, 3.1: 813-817.

Salonen, A. 1939. *Die Wasserfahrzeuge in Babylonien, nach sumerisch-akkadichen Quellen*. (Helsinki: Societas Orientalis Fennica)

Sandars N., 1985, *The Sea Peoples: Warriors of the Ancient Mediterranean, 1250-1150 B.C.*, (London: Thames and Hudson).

Scafoglio, G. 2004a. 'La questione ciclica', *Revue de philologie, de littérature et d'histoire anciennes*, 78.2: 289-310.

Scafoglio, G. 2004b 'Proclo e il ciclo epico', Göttinger Forum für Altertumswissenschaft, 7: 39-57.

Schachermeyr F., 1950, *Poseidon und die Enstehung des griechischen Götterglaubens*, (Bern: A. Francke AG Verlg)

Schäfer, M. 2005. 'The Greek Cavalry in the Archaic Period. A matter for review', in A. Gardeisen (ed) *Les Équidés Dans Le Monde Méditerranéen Antique: Actes Du Colloque Organisé Par L'Ecole Française D'Athènes, Le Centre Camille Jullian Et L'UMR 5140 Du CNRS, Athènes, 26-28 Novembre 2003*. (Rousillon: Éd. de l'Association pour le développement de l'archéologie en Languedoc), pp. 233-242.

Sciortino, G., Krueger M. 2009. 'Phoenicians and Greeks in the Western Mediterranean: Interpretations and Re-interpretations', *SOMA 2007: Proceedings of the XI Symposium on Mediterranean Archaeology, Istanbul Technical University, 24-29 April, 2007.* (Oxford: British Archaeological Reports Limited), p. 342

Shapland, A., Fitton J. L. 2019. 'Archaeological Troy', in A. Villing, J.L. Fitton, V. Donnellan, A. Shapland (eds), *Troy. Myth and Reality* (London: Thames and Hudson), pp. 126-181.

Sherrat, S. 2010a. 'The Trojan War: History or Bricolage?', *Bulletin of the Institute for Classical Studies*, 53.2: 1-18.

Sherrat, S. 2010b. 'Greeks and Phoenicians: perceptions of trade and traders in the early first millennium BC', *Social Archaeologies of Trade and Exchange: Exploring Relationships among People, Places, and Things*, pp. 119-42.

Snodgrass, A. 1998. *Homer and the artists: text and picture in early Greek art* (Cambridge University Press).

Sommer, M. 2008. *I Fenici* (Bologna: Il Mulino)

Sparkes, B. A. 1971. 'The Trojan Horse in Classical Art', *Greece & Rome*, 18.1: 54-70.

Stanford, W.B., Luce, J.W. 1974. *The quest for Ulysses.* (London: Phaidon/Praeger).

Stieglitz, R., 1999. 'Phoenician Ship equipment and fitting', *Tropis IV. 4th International Symposium on Ship Construction in Antiquity, Delphi*: 412.

Strauss, B. 2006, *The Trojan War. A new History*, (New York: Simon & Schuster Paperback).

Tadmor, H. 1958. 'The campaigns of Sargon II of Assur: a chronological-historical study', *Journal of Cuneiform Studies*, 12.1: 22-40.

Tartaron, T. F. 2013. Maritime connections in the Mycenaean world (Cambridge: Cambridge Unuversity Press).

Tchernia, André. 2001. 'Eustathe et le rafiot d'Ulysse (Od. V)', in J.P. Brun, P. Jockey (eds), *Technai -Techniques et sociétés en Méditeranée* (Aix-en-Provence:MMSH), pp. 625-631.

Tiboni, F. 2016. 'The Dourateos Ippos from allegory to Archaeology: a Phoenician Ship to break the Wall', *Archaeologia Maritima Mediterranea*,13: 91-104.

Tiboni, F. 2018. 'Per una rilettura delle navi di Glasinac', *Archaeologia Maritima Mediterranea*,15: 57-68.

Torr, C., 1896. *Ancient Ships* (Cambridge: Cambridge University Press).

Treziny, H. 1980. 'Navires attiques et navires corinthiens à la fin du VIIIe siècle [À propos d'un cratère géométrique de Mégara Hyblaea]'*Mélanges de l'Ecole française de Rome. Antiquité*, 92.1: 17-34

Uberti, M.L. 2005. *Introduzione alla storia del Vicino Oriente Antico* (Bologna: Il Mulino).

Van de Moortel, A. 2012. 'Middle Bronze Age Boat of Mitrou, Central Greece', in N. Günsenin (ed.), *Between Continents, Proceeding of 12th ISBSA, Istanbul 2009*, (Istanbul: Yayinlari), pp. 17-26.

Vian, F. 1959. *Recherches sur les Posthomerica de Quintus de Smyrne*, Etude et Commentaires, 30. (Paris: Klincksieck).

Vinson, S. 1994. *Egyptian Boats and Ships*, (Princes Reisborough: Shire).

Wachsmann, S. 1995. 'Paddled and Oared Ships Before the Iron Age', in R. Gardiner (ed). *The Age of the Galley. Mediterranean Oared vessels since Pre-Classical time* (London: Conway Maritime Press), pp. 10-35.

Wachsmann, S. 1998. *Seagoing ships seamanship of the Bronze Age Levant* (College Station: Texas A&M University Press).

Wäfler, M. 1975. *Nicht-Assyrer neuassyrischer Darstellungen*, 1 (Kevelaer: Butzon und Bercker).

Wallinga, T. H. 'The Ancestry of the Trireme 1200-525 BC', in R. Gardiner (ed). *The Age of the Galley. Mediterranean Oared vessels since Pre-Classical time* (London: Conway Maritime Press), pp. 36-48.

Walter, H.1962. *Mitteilungen des Deutschen Archäologischen Instituts*, LXXVII (Berlin: Deutsch. Arch. Inst. Athen.)

West, M.L. 2003. *Greek Epic Fragments from the 7th to the 5th centuries BC* (Harvard: Harvard University Press).

West, M.L. 2007. *Indo-European poetry and myth.* (Oxford: Oxford University Press).

West, M.L. 2013. *The Epic Cycle. A commentary on the Lost Troy Epics* (Oxford: Oxford University Press).

Whitley, J. 1991. *Style and society in the Dark Age Greece. The changing face a pre-literate society 1100-700 BC*, (Cambridge: Cambridge University Press).

Ancient authors

Apollonius Rhodius, *Argonautica.* Argonautica. Apollonius Rhodius. George W. Mooney. London. Longmans, Green. 1912.

Appian, *The Civil Wars.* The Civil Wars. Appian. Horace White. London. MACMILLAN AND CO., LTD. 1899.

Athenaeus. The Deipnosophists. with an English Translation by. Charles Burton Gulick. Cambridge, MA. Harvard University Press. London. William Heinemann Ltd. 1927. 1.

Catullus, *Carmina.* Catullus. The Carmina of Gaius Valerius Catullus. Leonard C. Smithers. London. Smithers. 1894.

Demosthenes, *Letters.* Demosthenes with an English translation by Norman W. DeWitt, Ph.D., and Norman J. DeWitt, Ph.D. Cambridge, MA, Harvard University Press; London, William Heinemann Ltd. 1949.

Euphorion of Calchis, *Fragments*, Meinke A., 1843, *De Euphorionis Chalcidensis vita e scriptis.* Analecta Alexandrina, Berlin.

Herodotus, *Histories.* Herodotus, with an English translation by A. D. Godley. Cambridge. Harvard University Press. 1920

Homer, The Odyssey. *Homer. The Odyssey with an English Translation by A.T. Murray, PH.D.* in two volumes. Cambridge, MA., Harvard University Press; London, William Heinemann, Ltd. 1919.

Homer, The Iliad. *Homer. The Iliad with an English Translation by A.T. Murray, Ph.D.* in two volumes. Cambridge, MA., Harvard University Press; London, William Heinemann, Ltd. 1924.

Horace, *Odes.* Horace. The Odes and Carmen Saeculare of Horace. John Conington. trans. London. George Bell and Sons. 1882.

Johannes Lydus, *De Mensibus.* John Lydos, *De Mensibus Of the Months*, translated by Andrew Eastburne for Roger Pearse in 2013.

Pausanias, *Description of Greece.* Pausanias. Pausanias Description of Greece with an English Translation by W.H.S. Jones, Litt.D., and H.A. Ormerod, M.A., in 4 Volumes. Cambridge, MA, Harvard University Press; London, William Heinemann Ltd. 1918.

Plautus, *Rudens.* The Comedies of Plautus. Henry Thomas Riley. London. G. Bell and Sons. 1912.

Pliny the Elder, The Natural History. Pliny the Elder. John Bostock, M.D., F.R.S. H.T. Riley, Esq., B.A. London. Taylor and Francis, Red Lion Court, Fleet Street. 1855.

Plutarch, *Parallel Lives. Marcellus.* Plutarch. Plutarch's Lives. with an English Translation by. Bernadotte Perrin. Cambridge, MA. Harvard University Press. London. William Heinemann Ltd. 1917. 5.

Quintus Smyrnaeus, *Posthomerica.* Quintus Smyrnaeus. The Fall of Troy. Arthur S. Way. London: William Heinemann; New York: G.P. Putnam's Sons. 1913.

Sophocles, *Thrachiniae*, The Women of Trachis and Philoctetes. A new translation in verse by Robert Torrance. Houghton Mifflin. 1966.

Sophocles, *Andromeda. Sophocles. Fragments of known Plays*, Loeb Classical Library, 1996.

Strabo, *Geography.* The Geography of Strabo. Literally translated, with notes, in three volumes. London. George Bell & Sons. 1903.

Tacitus, *Historiae.* Complete Works of Tacitus. Tacitus. Alfred John Church. William Jackson Brodribb. Sara Bryant. edited for Perseus. New York.: Random House, Inc. Random House, Inc. 1873. reprinted 1942.

Theocritus, *Idyllis.* Idylls. Theocritus. R. J. Cholmeley, M.A. London. George Bell & Sons. 1901.

Thucydides, *Peloponnesian War.* Thucydides. The Peloponnesian War. London, J. M. Dent; New York, E. P. Dutton. 1910.

Vergil, *Aeneid.* Vergil. Aeneid. Theodore C. Williams. trans. Boston. Houghton Mifflin Co. 1910.

Vitruvius, *De Architectura.* Vitruvius: The Ten Books on Architecture. Vitruvius. Morris Hicky Morgan. Cambridge: Harvard University Press. London: Humphrey Milford. Oxford University Press. 1914.

Xenophon. *Hellenica. Xenophon in Seven Volumes*, 1 and 2. Carleton L. Brownson. Harvard University Press, Cambridge, MA; William Heinemann, Ltd., London. vol. 1:1918; vol. 2: 1921.

Xenophon, *Economics. Xenophon. Xenophontis opera omnia*, vol. 2, 2nd ed. Oxford, Clarendon Press. 1921 (repr. 1971).